T0361286

Cambridge Elements ≡

Elements in the Philosophy of Immanuel Kant
edited by
Desmond Hogan
Princeton University
Howard Williams
University of Cardiff
Allen Wood
Indiana University

THE KANTIAN FEDERATION

Luigi Caranti
University of Catania

CAMBRIDGE
UNIVERSITY PRESS

CAMBRIDGE
UNIVERSITY PRESS

University Printing House, Cambridge CB2 8BS, United Kingdom

One Liberty Plaza, 20th Floor, New York, NY 10006, USA

477 Williamstown Road, Port Melbourne, VIC 3207, Australia

314–321, 3rd Floor, Plot 3, Splendor Forum, Jasola District Centre,
New Delhi – 110025, India

103 Penang Road, #05–06/07, Visioncrest Commercial, Singapore 238467

Cambridge University Press is part of the University of Cambridge.

It furthers the University's mission by disseminating knowledge in the pursuit of
education, learning, and research at the highest international levels of excellence.

www.cambridge.org
Information on this title: www.cambridge.org/9781009016971
DOI: 10.1017/9781009037013

First published 2022

A catalogue record for this publication is available from the British Library.

ISBN 978-1-009-01697-1 Paperback
ISSN 2397-9461 (online)
ISSN 2514-3824 (print)

The Kantian Federation

Elements in the Philosophy of Immanuel Kant

DOI: 10.1017/9781009037013
First published online: May 2022

Luigi Caranti
University of Catania
Author for correspondence: Luigi Caranti, lcaranti@unict.it

Abstract: This Element introduces the reader to Kant's theory of peace and to its place in the broader context of the critical philosophy. It also delves into one aspect of the model that has generated much debate among interpreters because of Kant's changing thoughts on the matter. This aspect relates to the nature and powers of the international federation. Defending the idea that national sovereignty is indissolubly linked to states' full autonomy regarding the use of military power, this Element offers an interpretation and defense of the Kantian federation that, in many regards, departs from the mainstream reading. Special emphasis is placed on the problematic coexistence of two conflicting theoretical desiderata: on the one hand, the necessity of establishing an international institution with coercive powers for securing peace; on the other hand, the necessity of avoiding the risk of an excessive erosion of states' sovereignty.

This Element also has a video abstract: www.cambridge.org/caranti

Keywords: peace, federalism, cosmopolitanism, international right, sovereignty

ISBNs: 9781009016971 (PB), 9781009037013 (OC)
ISSNs: 2397-9461 (online), 2514-3824 (print)

Contents

1 Introduction

Kant's theory of peace is likely the most popular part of his critical philosophy and certainly the one that reached the most diverse audiences, with an impact extending beyond the circle of interpreters or academics, a significant influence on policy makers, and concrete repercussions in the building of major regional and global institutions.[1] There are obvious reasons behind this popularity. One is the intrinsic importance of a philosophical project meant to overcome what Voltaire wittingly described as the self-inflicted human tragedy: war. Another is the attractiveness of a model based simply on three major reforms: (1) the overcoming of despotism through the republicanization of national regimes, (2) the building of a peace-promoting supranational institution, and (3) the recognition by all states of the cosmopolitan right of each human being to visit other states. Yet another reason is the style that Kant adopts, significantly more direct and enjoyable than the one reserved for the three critiques. When one takes a closer look, however, the model reveals a number of puzzles, problems, and difficulties: some long debated among generations of Kant scholars, others less analyzed but relevant to conceptualizing some important political issues of our world.

This Element has two major goals. On the one hand, it introduces the reader to Kant's theory of peace and to the way in which it fits within the broader context of the critical philosophy (Sections 1–3). On the other hand, it digs into one aspect of the model related to the "federalism of free states" (ZeF 8:354), an aspect that has generated much debate among Kant interpreters, given its centrality to the entire project and Kant's changing attitude toward the nature and the powers of the supranational institution that he advocates as a necessary ingredient of his model (Sections 4–8). The Element offers an interpretation of the Kantian federation that in many regards departs from the mainstream reading. Special emphasis will be placed on the problematic coexistence of two conflicting theoretical desiderata: on the one hand, the necessity of establishing an international institution, either in the form of a world republic or a federal state with coercive powers, for *securing* peace; on the other hand, the necessity of avoiding the risk of an excessive erosion of states' sovereignty.

These two major goals will be pursued in seven steps. In the first and second sections, the Element illustrates Kant's project of perpetual peace. Kant thought

---

[1] The present work expands and, where necessary, modifies my views of Kant's model for peace as offered in a number of publications (Caranti 2014, 2016, 2017a, 2017b, 2018). A few passages from those works have been reproduced without major changes. References to Kant's works follow the abbreviations adopted by the Kant Gesellschaft. For a list see www.kant-gesellschaft.de/en/ks/Hinweise_Autoren_2018.pdf. The English translation of Kant's works is that of the Cambridge edition.

that if we want to abolish forever interstate wars we need to globally implement three major institutional reforms: At the domestic level, all states should overcome despotism and become republican (in a sense that will be explained in due course); at the international level, all states should enter a supranational institution meant at the very least to serve as a forum for handling controversies peacefully; and at the cosmopolitan level, all states should recognize the right to visit on the part of foreigners entering their territory. These three reforms are the object of the three "definitive articles," the backbone of Kant's entire project. During the process leading to a global implementation of these reforms, political leaders should follow six additional rules that Kant calls "preliminary articles," mainly meant to decrease the likelihood of war and keep international relation above a certain degree of civility, so that that very transition does not prove too difficult. Kant complements his project with two supplements and an appendix in two parts. Since excellent commentaries on *Toward Perpetual Peace* already exist, I will mention the essentials of the project and quickly move to the discussion of its most problematic and fascinating aspects, particularly those still in need of interpretive clarification.[2] Among these are: (a) the far-reaching theoretical consequences of the "division of work" between preliminary and definitive articles in terms of what we would today call non-ideal and ideal theory; (b) the ensuing survival in the model of some space for just war theory despite Kant's harsh criticism of the "sorry comforters" (ZeF 8:355) Grotius, Pufendorf, and Vattel; (c) the probabilistic nature of the argument resting on citizens' aversion to war (Caranti 2017a, Guyer 2006); (d) the question of whether only republics or any kinds of states are allowed to become members (Caranti 2017a, Cavallar 2015, Doyle 1983a, b, MacMillan 1995, Rawls 1999); and (e), the question of whether cosmopolitan right (the right to visit) is supposed to contribute to the cause of peace by merely enabling international economic interdependence or, more broadly, by fostering peoples' reciprocal knowledge and understanding.

The third section focuses on the place of Kant's peace project in the architectonic of the critical philosophy. I will address the question of compatibility between some aspects of the model and Kant's epistemological and moral commitments as presented in the three critiques. On the one hand, the focus will be on Kant's idea that nature "guarantees" that humankind, willingly or unwillingly, will reach a global durable peace. This thesis will be defended – to the extent that this is possible – in the face of three major challenges – epistemological, moral, and anthropological – raised against it (Caranti 2014, Eberl and Niesen 2011, Guyer 2006, Ludwig 2006). On the other hand, the

---

[2] Two recent thorough commentaries are Byrd and Hruschka (2010) and Eberl and Niesen (2011).

focus will be on the relationship between knowledge, morality, and politics. It will be highlighted how Kant interprets politics as relatively independent of morality, prescribing that politicians (*especially* the moral ones) interpret their role as irreducible to a mechanical application of the principles of right to the complexity of human affairs. It will be shown that moral politicians need to avoid two opposite and yet equally dangerous epistemological excesses: on the one hand, the disregard for the repercussions of their pursuing justice in a specific context, fueled by an acritical endorsement of the "*fiat justitia, pereat mundus* [Let justice be done, though the world perish]" maxim; on the other hand, the ultimately paralyzing attempt to predict with any degree of precision the consequences of one's political initiative, an ambition that merely mimics the responsible attitude of the moral politician while in reality it turns out to be closer to a technical understanding of politics that Kant rejects and attributes to what he calls "political moralists."

After having illustrated Kant's project of perpetual peace and discussed its place in the critical system, Sections 4–8 focus on international right, with the second definitive article's prescription to build a "federalism of free states" (ZeF 8:354); that is, an international federation among states to overcome – at least to a certain extent – the lawless, hence war-prone condition of international relations. Section 3 reconstructs the evolution of Kant's thought on international right. A textual analysis will show how Kant reshapes the notion of international right itself over time, with a major breakthrough in *Toward Perpetual Peace*. Moreover, it will be shown that Kant progressively abandons the idea of conceiving the exiting from the state of nature at the international level in strict analogy with the domestic case, and thus moves from a preference for the institution of a supranational institution with coercive powers, either in the form of a world state or in that of a state of states, to one based on normative, not merely empirical or pragmatic considerations, for a league of states without coercive powers.

Section 5 discusses the arguments Kant offers to justify his preference for the federation of nations (*Völkerbund*) over the state of nations (*Völkerstaat*). I will distinguish three lines of argument – empirical, logical, and moral – and will suggest that Kant's strongest argument in favor of the federation is the moral one, which turns on the moral personality of states, in turn ultimately resting on the freedom of citizens.

Section 6 confronts some of the most interesting readings on the federation *versus* world republic issue offered in the first two decades of the twenty-first century. I will focus on four major critics of Kant's preference for the federation over the ideal of the world republic: Thomas Pogge, Jürgen Habermas, Pauline Kleingeld, and Otfried Höffe. Independently of their differences, they all propose an "enhanced" league or minimal world republic as the kind of institution Kant either defended or should have defended, given the function the federation is supposed to play.

In replying to these critics in Section 7, I will suggest that: (a) Kant never abandoned the idea that the only true guarantor of peace is a world republic or a federation with coercive powers; (b) the reason why he ended up advocating for a voluntary league without coercive powers is not that he "did not/could not" think of the solution of breaking down sovereignty, with some competences transferred to a supranational institution and others kept for nation states; it is rather that he *correctly* saw that at least in the crucial area of using force toward external actors – the area that matters most for a theory of international peace – a state may not compromise on its *exclusive* competence, if it is to remain sovereign at all; c) Kant thus favored the solution of the voluntary league because he wanted to avoid the merging of all states into one, a goal shared also by those critics who reproach him for his lack of courage and/or consistency; (d) the league, while by itself not a guarantee, would still be a significant peace factor because it would offer a permanent channel of diplomatic relations where states have the chance to have their controversies discussed and assessed by something like a third, independent party – the partial overcoming of the international state of nature through a court recently highlighted by Ripstein (Ripstein 2009: 228); and (e), despite his preference for the federation, Kant never ruled out the possibility – in fact he kept hoping – that states might voluntarily choose to dissolve in order to enter a larger global institution.[3] Yet I will suggest that it is not entirely clear from a Kantian perspective how the transition should unfold without violating the basic rights of citizens who may oppose it.

Section 8 deals with the reading of Kant's international right offered by Katrin Flikschuh. This reading is consonant with our suggestion that states cannot divide up their sovereignty as easily as Habermas and so many others assume. Yet, in overlooking how this extends to the strict impossibility on the part of states to compromise on their exclusive competence to go to war, I will argue that Flikschuh does not get to the heart of the paradox Kant is facing.

Both the overview of Kant's theory of peace in Sections 2–3 and the relatively detailed analysis of international right offered in the remaining sections are carried out by staying close to Kant's text. This should enable readers to grasp the intricate and interesting problems that Kant's model reveals, despite its apparent simplicity.

---

[3] For a similar position see Cavallar (2020: 154, 159).

2 Kant's Project of Perpetual Peace

Zum Ewigen Frieden: Ein Philosophischer Entwurf, published in 1795, was probably the greatest literary success Kant had in his life. Shortly after its publication, translations in French and English appeared, and by around the end of the century the essay had gained centrality in the intellectual debate in France and Germany. By the time Kant died (nine years after the book's appearance), his "philosophical project" had reached its tenth edition. After that, its popularity started to decline. Probably the cosmopolitan orientation of the essay, meant as an antidote to the excesses of nationalism, as well as its ahistorical, abstract, universal definition of the just state displeased the taste of an increasingly Romantic intellectual milieu. After various ups and downs of fortune, with "returns to Kant" especially in the aftermath of the two world wars – when both the League of Nations and the United Nations were inspired by Kant's plea for a global federation – a number of factors, including the birth of democratic peace theory in the early 1980s; the fall of the Berlin Wall (with the subsequent third wave of democratization), and the occasion of the 200th anniversary of its publication gave the essay a new elan. Today, one can hardly dispute that Kant's project (or better, the mainstream interpretation of it) is part of the background knowledge not only of philosophers but also of international relations scholars, historians, political scientists, and, most importantly, political leaders of contemporary liberal democracies.

Kant articulates his project according to the structure typical of the international treaties of his time. We thus have preliminary and definitive articles, supplements, and a two-part appendix. Undoubtedly the definitive articles are the center of the entire work. Here Kant provides his "philosophical project" in favor of peace. The other parts, albeit peripheral, are crucial for a proper understanding of the definitive articles themselves.

2.1 The Preliminary Articles

At the beginning of the essay Kant lists and briefly discusses six preliminary articles. They express obligations that heads of state should follow either strictly (*leges strictae*) or with some latitude as to the time of implementation (*leges latae*). Their main point is to ensure that some major factors generating hostility among states are removed. They are as follows:

1. No treaty of peace shall be held to be such if it is made with a secret reservation of material for a future war. (ZeF 8:343)
2. No independently existing state (whether small or large) shall be acquired by another state through inheritance, exchange, purchase, or donation. (ZeF 8:344)

3. Standing armies (*miles perpetuus*) shall in time be abolished altogether. (ZeF 8:345)
4. No national debt shall be contracted with regard to the external affairs of a state. (ZeF 8:345)
5. No state shall forcibly interfere in the constitution and government of another state. (ZeF 8:346)
6. No state at war with another shall allow itself such acts of hostility as would have to make mutual trust impossible during a future peace; acts of this kind are employing assassins (*percussores*) or poisoners (*venefici*), breach of surrender, incitement to treason (*perduellio*) within the enemy state, and so forth. (ZeF 8:346)

A good part of the hermeneutical challenge posed by these articles has to do with a precise understanding of the sense in which they are "preliminary." Prima facie they seem to be guidelines that responsible, moral rulers should follow *before the reforms spelled out in the definitive articles are fully implemented.*[4] They make the transition to the world envisaged by the three definitive articles as easy as possible, or perhaps, more modestly, they ensure that, while waiting for the realization of the three definitive articles, the situation does not worsen to a point of no return. As such, they recall the tradition of natural law, strongly interested in introducing some elements of lawfulness into the otherwise lawless context par excellence; that is, war (*inter arma enim silent leges*).

But here comes the first interpretative problem. Kant ridicules the work of Grotius, Pufendorf, and Vattel, whom he dismisses as "sorry comforters" because they propose precepts to make the waging and the conduct of war (*ius ad bellum* and *ius in bello*, respectively) less lawless and arbitrary, as opposed to finding solutions that will prevent all wars in the first place. And yet one may legitimately wonder whether the preliminary articles are meant to do anything different from what Kant had bitterly reproached them for. To be sure, in one sense preliminary articles are different. They are not merely counsels aimed at making war *less arbitrary* from a moral point of view. Their main point is rather that of making war *less likely*. Even the recommendations such as the prohibition against using assassins and poisoners within an enemy state (article 6), which may appear as inspired by humanitarian preoccupations, are rather explicitly meant to prevent the breach of any confidence between enemies "during a future peace" (ZeF 8:346). This is an entirely

---

[4] Eberl and Niesen distinguish three distinct phases in the evolution toward a global legal condition: the state of nature among states, a transitory phase, and finally public international right (Eberl and Niesen 2011: 100–1, 129). The second phase corresponds to a time in which the preliminary articles are implemented to some extent.

different perspective, one that squares perfectly with the essay's general orientation, in line with a tradition of thought – that of the peace treaties – different from and concurrent with that of the natural law; this is precisely because the former, unlike the latter, aims to abolish war, not to legalize or humanize it.[5] Moreover, while for the authors of the natural law tradition the regulation of an otherwise lawless reality was the end point of the project, for Kant it is nothing but a preparatory stage, very much as an anesthetic is merely the preparation for surgery aiming at the eradication of an illness. To continue with the metaphor, there is nothing wrong in relieving patients from immediate, acute suffering by using painkillers, thereby making them better able to endure the necessary treatment. But limiting one's therapeutic strategy to palliatives is at best ineffective and at worst counterproductive in that it delays the identification – let alone the solution – of the problem.

Having said that, it would be a serious mistake to downplay the importance of these articles and to consider them as entirely dispensable, even if the three definitive articles are fully and globally implemented. It is important to realize that even in this case, the preliminary articles would still have a role, because, as we shall see, in the final version of Kant's project even the implementation of the three definitive articles will *not* yield a condition in which war is truly abolished. To anticipate a point that will be discussed in some detail in the last four sections of this Element, Kant's mature preference for a voluntary league with no coercive powers, rather than a world republic or a federation with coercive powers, implies the acceptance that the state of nature at the international level is never completely overcome. Indeed, Kant is very clear – and he never changed his mind about this – that the only true guarantor of peace is a state of states or a world republic. But since he rejects this solution in favor of a voluntary league (for reasons that we will discuss in due course), it follows that even if all states are republics, there is a voluntary league among them, and the right to visit is globally respected, there is no guarantee that conflicts will not re-emerge somewhere. As he puts it, the "surrogate" of the federation "can hold back the stream of hostile inclination that shies away from right, though with constant danger of its breaking out" (ZeF 8:357). In the *Metaphysics of Morals* he repeats the point even more clearly, saying that the impossibility of creating a world state is the reason why "*perpetual peace*, the ultimate goal of the whole right of nations, is indeed an unachievable idea" (MS 6:350). If this is the case, the preliminary articles will never go out of fashion, so to speak.

With this in mind we can perhaps address a point that has recently generated a good amount of controversy among interpreters. This concerns the very

---

[5] See on this Archibugi (1995).

survival of just war theory in Kant's thought. On the one hand, at least one preliminary article of *Toward Perpetual Peace* (the sixth, see above in Section 2.1) seems to be fully in the natural law tradition that Kant ridicules. Moreover, and most importantly, as particularly emphasized by a recent commentary (Eberl and Niesen 2011), there are sections in the *Metaphysics of Morals* where Kant gives very serious consideration to the eighteenth-century views in international law which permit wars in self-defense, even *pre-emptive* ones (*ius ad bellum*) (MS 6:346), as well as to prevalent contemporary views on moral conduct during war (*ius in bello*) (MS 6:347) and after war (*ius post bellum*) (MS 6:348–9). Byrd and Hruschka think that "Kant's position in the *Doctrine of Right* on the right to wage war is exactly the opposite to his position in *Perpetual Peace* where he says 'a right to wage war' is unconceivable" (Byrd and Hruschka 2010: 194–5). The survival of these elements is problematic not only because Kant scorns the "sorry comforters" but also because, as recently noticed by Ripstein, one may wonder "how Kant can have a conception of right in war against the background of his more general view that war is by its nature barbaric and to be repudiated entirely" (Ripstein 2016, 180). Ripstein's solution is that Kant innovates over what he calls the regular war tradition and the just war tradition by claiming that, in a dispute between two states, no claim may be put forward in which one party assumes itself to be in the right because there is really no higher impartial authority that can decide on the matter. States cannot appeal to a moral or legal universal code to claim they are on the side of justice, because by doing so they would be simultaneously prosecutors, judges, and executioners in their own cases. And yet, since they incarnate a rightful public condition, however defective, they can still appeal to right to justify their recourse to violence. In particular – Ripstein seems to suggest – state A can require from other states all sets of actions and omissions evidently necessary to have its juridical condition, which minimally includes its existence and independence, respected. For example, if threatened or attacked by another state they have a right to self-defense (*ius ad bellum*), they have a rightful claim that acts of hostility that would make "mutual trust impossible during a future peace" be banned (*ius in bello*), and they have a right to be assured that "the victor will not impose compensation for the costs of the war" (*ius post bellum*), because this would imply that other states are entitled to judge the moral quality of the war fought by A, while only a third independent party is entitled to make this judgment.[6]

---

[6] In his more recent *Rules for Wrongdoers* (2021), Ripstein further develops this idea by arguing that even if there is an *ius ad bellum* (an attacked state still has a right to defend itself, although this should not be viewed, as the tradition suggests, as a compensatory or remedial war), this is fully

I am not sure that Ripstein's suggestion holds. If there is no third independent party, who is entitled to judge whether, for example, a certain act disables mutual trust or disrespects other states' independence? Still, his analysis nicely illuminates a problem with which Kant evidently struggles. Hence, I would complement his suggestion by expanding a point we already made. There are three main reasons why a theory of the morality of war survives in Kant. To begin with, since a full implementation of the three definitive articles is still to be reached (and probably never will be reached without some shortcoming or imperfection in one of the three dimensions), we are still in the condition whereby war may break out at any time. Secondly, even if one day the three definitive articles are fully implemented, humanity may (at least for some time) experience setbacks. Republics may fall back to despotism, states may abandon the global federation, states may stop recognizing the right of foreigners to visit them. Finally, and more profoundly, the mature Kant rejects the solution of a world republic, which by his own standards would be the sole true guarantee of peace. As we shall see, the normative price to pay, that is, the melting of all states into one, would be too high. All this generates an intrinsically precarious condition that means the normative precepts on the morality of war are always valid. Considerations concerning when one can recur to interstate violence, how war should be conducted, and what to do when the conflict is over, are never – and unfortunately never likely will be – outdated. There is no contradiction between having a theory that spells out the conditions that make war less and less likely and keeping a suboptimal theory of the morality of war, given its residual possibility.

Much more could be said about the preliminary articles. For example, the prohibition of standing armies is intriguing. By that Kant means professional forces (either composed of citizens or foreign mercenaries), contrasting them with a system of conscription. Kant was mainly worried that the existence of professional forces may incentivize a race among states to have the strongest army. But there is an additional, perhaps even more important point. Republican citizens may find a war advantageous if they have hired professionals to do the fighting. This would risk undermining the whole first definitive article, whose logic, as we shall see in a moment, is that republics are more peace prone because in a republican system those who make the decisions (citizens) want to avoid the hardships of war. After the repeated experience of contractors, especially in Afghanistan and in Iraq, today we know that a further complication is the creation and expansion of a war industry that again risks defusing the

---

independent of the *ius in bello*. Both sides (aggressor and victim) have to conduct war in a manner (avoidance of perfidy, for example) that does not remove the possibility of a future peace.

peace potential of the first definitive article. Those (privately) interested in the material advantages of war are well positioned to exploit citizens' confidence that the fighting will not touch them or their nearest and dearest. The case of the 2003 Iraq war is telling: Recall Dick Cheney, and the huge profits made by the contracting company Halliburton for which he had worked until taking office, and from which he allegedly kept receiving remuneration while in office.[7]

Let us also pause on the fifth preliminary article, because it helps to complete the picture of Kant's model in a way that could hardly be obtained by looking merely at the definitive articles. Given two states, A and B, the fifth article forbids A's interference in B's internal affairs, even if B looks "scandalous" to A; that is, if the injustice perpetrated in B by the rulers arouses feelings of solidarity for the victims among the citizens of A. Kant here condemns any sort of crusade led by "virtuous" states (the "republican" or "liberal- democratic" ones) against despotic regimes.[8] The overthrowing of despotism cannot result from the initiative of republican states more or less sincerely interested in the affirmation of justice outside of their borders. Only from the perspective of impersonal spectators can we rejoice in the removal of a dictatorship and the rise of a new "republic," which is, in fact, precisely what Kant does regarding the French Revolution (SF 7:85). In short, this refutes the crusade model that certain realist authors (and self-interested politicians) have construed and attempted to pass as inspired by Kant.[9] At the same time, however, the article authorizes external intervention in cases in which a country is so divided that it can no longer guarantee a juridical condition. Whether this makes Kant's theory compatible with, or even attuned to the principles of the contemporary responsibility to protect, as some argue (Roff 2015), is a theme for debate. Certainly it is Kant's considered position that if a state falls into barbarism; that is, into a condition of force without law and freedom, as per the definition of the *Anthropology* (Anth 7:331), then an intervening state does no wrong, not because the conditions are outrageous enough to license intervention, but because there is no juridical condition to respect. It is also true, however, that for Kant nothing could be done against states that are *not* so divided but yet commit humanitarian offenses that the responsibility-to-protect doctrine considers as sufficient for triggering intervention, up to its most serious form, that is, the military one.[10]

---

[7] See Rosenbaum (2004).

[8] According to Losurdo (1983), one of the goals of the rule of noninterference stated in the fifth preliminary article, which, significantly, had already appeared in the 1793 French constitution, was to protect France from external reactionary forces that wanted to restore the *ancien régime*.

[9] For a criticism of these attempts see Caranti (2006) and Russett (2005).

[10] To recall, the threshold is: "large scale loss of life, actual or apprehended, with genocidal intent or not, which is the product either of deliberate state action, or state neglect or inability to act, or

Finally, something should be said about articles 1 and 4. Clearly they are both rather vulnerable to criticism inspired by experience. Regarding article 1, it is easy for states to walk away from a signed treaty by claiming that the other parties have some secret reservation. Precisely because the alleged reservation is secret, one would have a hard time obtaining evidence of the existence of such a reservation. Regarding article 4, one might suspect that the prohibition against borrowing to fund aggressive plans in foreign policy could be easily overcome. The state might be using the money it obtains from regular revenues for its aggressive plans while using the money it has borrowed for domestic affairs (welfare, administration of justice, the police, and so on).[11] This offers us the opportunity to complete the point we made earlier about preliminary articles in general. They are rules meant to decrease the likelihood of war. Significant as they might be, they are not, and were never meant to be, solutions to the problem of war. In addition, we can now take notice of the following: While the definitive articles are derived directly from pure practical reason and remain valid independently of empirical considerations (for even if factually we were to discover that republics are not more peace prone than despotic regimes, the prescription that we should approximate our state to republican standards would still be valid), the preliminary articles are inspired by past experience and are as good as the reasons we hold for believing that they will deliver the result they promise.

2.2 The First Definitive Article

The first definitive article contains the prescription that each and every state should become "republican." It reads: "The civil constitution in every state shall be republican" (ZeF 8:349). Three main features characterize a republican constitution: the *freedom* of each member of society; the *dependence* of everyone upon a single and unified legislation; and legal *equality* for everyone; that is, nondiscrimination before the law. Three additional requirements are: (a) the people must hold legislative power; (b) rulers must legislate by interpreting the general will; and (c) there must be a sharp distinction of powers – in particular, the legislative is to be well separated from the executive (ZeF 8:352). These constitutional features are thought to be relevant to the cause of peace because only in a republic can the people influence the decision of whether the state should go to war.[12] Since citizens would suffer from the atrocities of a violent

---

a failed state situation; or large scale 'ethnic cleansing,' actual or apprehended, whether carried out by killing, forced expulsion, acts of terror or rape" (ICISS 2001, 32).

[11] Thanks to Thomas Pogge for drawing my attention to these points.

[12] One may object that while people in a republic hold legislative power, the decision to wage war is usually made by the executive. This is true but of limited significance. To begin with, in most

conflict, there is reason to believe that they "will be very hesitant to begin such a bad game" (ZeF 8:351). The opposite is the case for a despotic regime. The despot here is not a fellow citizen, but the owner of the state. As such, he can wage war with great ease, because he "gives up nothing at all of his feasts, hunts, pleasure palaces, court festivals, and so forth" (ZeF 8:351). The despot, Kant goes on, can thus "decide upon war, as upon a kind of pleasure party, for insignificant cause, and can with indifference leave the justification of the war, for the sake of propriety, to the diplomatic corps, which is always ready to provide it" (ZeF 8:351).

Some points in this apparently linear argument need to be clarified. First of all, Kant does not say that it is *impossible* that citizens will choose to embark on a bellicose adventure. He merely says that it is *unlikely* (Guyer 2006). The first article leaves open the possibility that democratic citizens, after due reflection, might find the costs of war worthwhile. Security, greed, national pride, or some combination of these factors can outweigh the cost a people is expected to pay. This leads to the second point: The logic Kant is using in this context is merely utilitarian. As far as the first article is concerned, the republican people can be as attracted by violence (and by the gains one can attain through it) as any other kind of people (or despot). Of course, Kant does believe that good/just institutions help the morality of citizens (IaG 8:21, 26; ZeF 8:366), which – one would think – implies that citizens learn to resist the impulse to use violence against other peoples to advance their interests. But, *at this stage of the argument*, Kant has still attributed to democratic peoples no deontological opposition to war. Kant's point can thus be reduced to this: As long as there is an owner of the state, there will not be a careful cost–benefit calculus that at least forestalls "inefficient" wars. But the first article leaves room for wars in the interest of republican peoples. After all, as history has abundantly shown, sometimes a republican or democratic people (or a large majority thereof) strongly desire war.

A closely related point completes said the argument we have made about the second preliminary article. If a republic's army is professional, let alone mainly made up of private contractors, the cost–benefit calculation will more easily favor war than in a case in which the army is based on conscription. Instead of considering whether we or our nearest and dearest will have to risk our lives on the battlefield, we, as republican citizens, are asked to make the

---

liberal democracies (probably the best approximation we have to Kantian republics), the executive decision (especially that of entering war) must be endorsed by parliament. Secondly, as I have explained elsewhere at length (Caranti 2022), for Kant even executive decisions – that is, decrees as opposed to laws – must ultimately reflect the general will, which in turn is obviously nothing but the will of people, in ideal circumstances.

considerably easier calculation of whether the costs of this semi- or fully private army amount to a good investment, all things considered.

The conclusion is that a republican government is by itself no assurance of peace. Contrary to what one sometimes reads (Archibugi and Beetham 1998), Kant did *not* believe that the problem of war could be reduced to a question of the right domestic institutions. The first definitive article, without the other two, does not guarantee *anything*, not even the elimination of conflicts between republics. That Kant's project presupposes the convergence of many peace-inducing factors, of which the internal republican constitution is only one, is a point as trivial as it is largely forgotten.

One less trivial point, equally overlooked, is that Kant's confidence in the pacific tendency of republics is to be read without passing in silence over his general distrust of democracy. Kant takes great care to make sure that "a republican constitution will not be confused with a democratic constitution (as usually happens)" (ZeF 8:351–2). Indeed, he thinks that in a democracy – at least in a democracy "in the strict sense of the word" (8:352) – despotism inevitably takes root. What Kant means by "democracy in the strict sense of the word," and why it should lead inevitably to despotism is not clear. He only offers two dense passages. On the one hand, he says, democracy "establishes an executive power in which all decide for and, if need be, against one (who thus does not agree), so that all, who are nevertheless not all, decide; and this is a contradiction of the general will with itself and with freedom" (ZeF 8:352). On the other hand, he praises the proclaimed attitude of Frederick II, who saw himself as the "servant of the state" – an emphatic way of saying that the supreme ruler makes decisions from the general will's perspective – only to point out that in a democracy this attitude on the part of political actors is impossible and the system is bound to be despotic. This is so, Kant says, "because there everyone wants to be ruler" (ZeF 8:353).

Byrd and Hruschka claim that the reason why democracy is always despotism is that if "the executive power is in the hands of all then there is no one left to hold the legislative power and the two cannot conceivably be separate" (Byrd and Hruschka 2010, 178). The dangerous overlapping between legislators and governors would happen only in a direct democracy where, literally, executive power (like the legislative) is in the hands of all. But in "representative" democracies, only a few can be elected governors. Hence, the problem of the necessary overlapping of those who hold legislative and executive power does not arise. Indeed, Byrd and Hruschka think that what we today call representative democracy is Kant's ideal form of state (Byrd and Hruschka 2010, 167).

Unfortunately, things are not so easy. Even if Byrd and Hruschka are correct that the abovementioned overlapping would by necessity only take place in direct democracies, the problem Kant detects is deeper. Kant's main concern is that democracies make decisions against single individuals without their consent, and this obviously happens in representative democracies too. Of course, much depends on what we mean by "without their consent." This might apply when people disagree because their interests are damaged (or they think this to be the case), even if the general good is served. This case would not be problematic. But at times, representative democracies violate the legitimate interests of some citizens (with or without their explicit consent) simply because some citizens manage to use their predominant influence to put in place laws that serve their interests even at the costs of violating the interests of others. In these cases, all too familiar in our time of rampant inequality and of the degeneration of democracy toward plutocracy (Gilens and Page 2017), the sheer separation of powers is no guarantee that an elected body of legislators will not rule "against" some citizens. Kant's reservations are not valid for direct democracies only.

What, then, is the real problem with democracy (of all kinds)? We need to clarify (a) why democracy – at least democracy in the truest sense of the word – establishes an executive power in which all citizens may make decisions about and indeed against one individual, (b) why this leads to a contradiction of the general will with itself (and with freedom), and (c) why every citizen's desire to be a ruler displays an attitude diametrically opposed to Frederick II's style of ruling as a servant of the state.

a. According to some interpreters (Pinzani 2008, Byrd and Hruschka 2010), Kant's model of democracy is ancient Athens. Therefore, the point that all citizens may make decisions against one individual may be taken as a reference to ostracism; that is, the practice of forcing individuals considered as dangerous (often mere political opponents, as in the case of Themistocles) out of the city. Even if this is true, we still need to understand what's wrong with democratic decisions similar to or modeled on ostracism. The problem cannot be the sheer dissent of the targeted (ostracized) individuals, because, of course, many rightful political decisions genuinely taken with the general good in mind will meet the de facto dissent of some individuals. One reasonable reading is that, as in the case of ostracism of political opponents, a decision by a faction *is masked as a decision taken by the whole people*, or as capable of expressing "the view of the city as a whole." While a king or an oligarchy must justify any decision taken against an individual as taken with the common good in mind, with a democratic vote, the urgency of such a justification diminishes. It is not a restricted circle that does the ostracizing. It is the *whole people* (or a majority of them) who make that call, and this by itself is taken as a sufficient justification. The problem with this condition is evident. No matter how far it is backed by popular support, a partisan decision masked as a decision made "by the whole city," or from the general will's perspective, is still a partisan, hence illegitimate decision.

b. The reading just offered would also help us to understand Kant's very cryptic point that decisions made by a democratic executive power (necessarily? possibly?) generate a contradiction of the general will with itself (and with freedom). The people, merely because they are supposed to be the *whole* people, take themselves as the infallible interpreters of the general will. And yet, since partisan decisions are possible even if everybody votes (according to Rousseau even if everybody agrees – *la volonté des tous*), what was supposed to be a decision taken from the perspective of the general will may very well be in contradiction with it. Finally, since any partisan decision will impact illegitimately on the freedom of one or more individuals, also freedom will be "contradicted"; that is, the innate right to freedom Kant attributes to individuals as their sole innate right will be violated.

c. Kant's concern that in a democracy "everybody wants to be a ruler [*Alles da Herr sein will*]," and that this creates an attitude opposed to the disposition to serve the general good attributed to Frederick II, adds a further and illuminating dimension to the problems identified so far. At first sight, one can hardly perceive an intrinsic flaw in each citizen's desire to be a ruler. What's wrong with my ambition to be a ruler, if I am ready to concede as legitimate the same ambition to all other citizens, as happens in a democratic system? The problem cannot be that each citizen is called to give his or her best interpretation of the general will, because this is what must happen with every ruling body, given Kant's standards, independent of whether they are made up of one, few, or all. What Kant seems to fear – at least this appears to me to be the sole plausible reading – is that in a democracy *all tend or are expected to represent their own interests only.*[13] This creates an attitude incompatible with the feature that should characterize the act of ruling, namely interpreting as well as possible the general will. While in a democracy I represent my will or that of my group, or even the will of

---

[13] An alternative reading could be that in a democracy each person wants to have something like the power of an oligarch or monarch: They feel empowered by their share in sovereignty and imagine they have more than is actually accorded by a democratically equal share. But this reading does not square with Kant's idea that democracy is *necessarily* despotism. If citizens exercise power correctly, that is, trying to rule from the general will's perspective, it does not matter whether they misperceive their share of power. They would be delusional about their power and yet good rulers, like Frederick II, according to Kant's standards.

all citizens if they happen to agree (Rousseau's *la volonté de tous*), the only thing that a republican ruler is bound to represent is the general will.[14]

Notice again the difference with the other two forms of sovereignty. While in the case of a monarchy or an oligarchy one can at least hope that political authority is inspired by a sincere attempt to interpret the general will, and in any event the ruling class must explain how decisions serve the general good, in a democracy, so understood at least, this hope would be ill-placed and the expectation that one will be given an explanation ungrounded. Citizens are *allowed, if not expected,* to represent themselves only. In fact, they don't even need to justify their decisions as arising from an attention to the common good, in the way a king or an oligarchy in a constitutional system must do. In voicing their preferences as representing only their private interests, they need offer no explanation. By mistaking the sum of all private wills for the general will, or even more grossly the will of the majority for the general will, democratic citizens think that anything they choose is right. Actually, Kant thinks, the greater the number of people who hold power, the less likely it is they will remember the burden of representation – a burden that no political power, not even that "of the people by the people," can escape.

This peculiarly democratic "perversion" – by the light of Kant's argument – is inevitable if we are dealing with a direct democracy. In this case, literally every citizen is allowed, if not expected, to voice his or her particular set of interests. But, less obviously (and in fact this is seldom if ever noticed), the same also holds also in a "representative" democracy, understood as a system based on the election of delegates. It does not matter whether democracy works through "representatives." For Kant, a system is not "representative" because it has delegates and a parliament where they meet. A system is representative when rulers (no matter how numerous they are and no matter where, how, and how often they meet) do not represent sectarian interests but make decisions with the common good as their *sole* guidance.[15] Even less obviously – and in fact, to my

---

[14] In contemporary scholarship, representation is often conceptualized differently. For example, Urbinati emphasizes advocacy of specific interests as an essential component of representation. However, she differentiates between advocacy and mere partisanship (Urbinati 2000, 775).

[15] Interestingly, this "uneasy alliance" between democracy and representation is at the center of two classical studies of representation from the past century, Pitkin's *The Concept of Representation* (1967) and Manin's *The Principles of Representative Government* (1997). For both Pitkin and Manin certain undemocratic, inegalitarian elements were key to the good functioning of a representative system and representative democracies had to be conceived ultimately as elective aristocracies. Political decisions always had to transcend the will of the people, understood as an aggregation of preferences. A similar point is made by scholars like Gutmann and Thompson (2004), who defend deliberative democracy; that is, the idea that citizens or their representatives owe each other mutually acceptable reasons for the laws they enact. Notice, though, that for Kant what is important is not whether the reasons we give each

knowledge, this has never been observed – this remains true even if a majority acts within constitutional limits. A constitutionally scrupulous political power may very well enact laws that protect the interests of some, instead of serving the general good.

This criticism of democracy is obviously compatible with the fact, quite well established in history before and after Kant, that monarchy and oligarchy serve partisan interests (those of the ruling family or group) more often and more effectively than democracy. When Kant claims that democracy "necessarily" leads to despotism, we need to understand the point not as an empirical generalization, but as a way of pinpointing a degeneration (partisanship accepted as political strategy) to which democracy is naturally exposed, given its tendency to accept competition between different interests and groups as the essence of politics.

If all this is correct, the Kantian–Rousseauian republic is a system in which no parliamentary majority, merely in virtue of the fact of being a majority, can enact partisan laws that are discriminatory against some citizens. In order to avoid a despotic degeneration, it is not sufficient that majorities respect constitutional limits. If they do, and yet ordinary laws and decrees shape a society that some citizens might not consent to (not even in principle), the laws (all kinds of laws) are no longer "absolutely *incapable* of doing anyone injustice" and the prepolitical entitlements of human beings (their right to an equal share of external freedom) are violated.[16]

This should help us to see why Kant is so suspicious of democracy, but it should also help us to conceive a form of democratic regime that does not run the risks Kant foresees. If the supreme law and the spirit of republicanism have shaped the minds of the citizens in such a way that they elect representatives with a clear mandate to issue laws not only formally consistent with the constitution but also capable of furthering the principles there expressed – if, in other words, the "burden of representation" is accepted by electors and elected – then there is no reason why a democracy could not be republican.[17] Actually, if care for the general good is embedded in the polity, democracy has a clear advantage over the other two *formae imperii*. As Kant says, these two forms "are always defective" because the executive power is exercised by one or a few, who by definition cannot represent all. Especially if they are not

---

other are mutually accepted but whether those laws *objectively* reflect the common good. For an updated overview of the current debate on representation, see Brito Vieira (2017).

[16] On Kant's theory of innate rights, see Caranti (2012).

[17] This is roughly the idea, inspired by Rawls, of "Legitimation by Constitution," defended in a forthcoming volume by Alessandro Ferrara and Frank I. Michelman (Ferrara and Michelman 2021).

elected, let alone unchecked by constitutional limits, one can at most hope that they freely choose to exercise their power in the right way. By contrast, in a republican democracy citizens vote on and influence political power and make sure that rulers further the general good and accept the burden of representation.

Important as this may be, it remains true that the logic of the first definitive article is a merely consequentialist one. Citizens will veto those wars that do not further the general good, something that is clearly compatible with the possibility that an aggressive foreign policy does further the general good of a specific nation. The cost–benefit calculation may suggest that war is in the best interest of a demos, not merely in the interests of absolute despots who use the lives of their subjects and resources of their countries to further their plans. To be sure, the argument could be made that citizens who have been socialized for long enough in the context of only republican institutions, and are hence habituated to deliberately taking into consideration the interests and rights of all fellow citizens (not only their own), will oppose "convenient" wars that are against the interests and rights of other human beings. Yet nothing in the way on which Kant explains the first definitive article suggests this further deontological argument. Without the other two articles, the first is limited to halting a bellicose attitude that is against the general good of a particular country.

2.3 The Second Definitive Article

The second definitive article contains the following prescription: "The right of nations shall be based on a *federalism* of free states" (ZeF 8:354). Here Kant envisages an institution that enables the diverse nations to overcome the anarchical state, or as it is usually referred to, "state of nature" which, by and large, still characterizes international relations. The transition resembles the move of individuals from the state of nature to the civil condition, but the analogy has its limits. For Kant, established states, unlike individuals in the state of nature, are already rightful entities whose autonomy is to be respected. For this reason, they cannot be forced to give up their sovereignty. As he puts it, "as states, they already have a rightful constitution internally and hence have outgrown the constraint of others to bring them under a more extended law-governed constitution in accordance with their concepts of right" (ZeF 8:356). But since reason dictates the duty to achieve peace, and peace requires "a pact of nations among themselves," it follows that "there must be a league of a special kind, which can be called a *pacific league* (*foedus pacificum*)" (ZeF 8:356).

Among the many interpretative challenges posed by the second definitive article, two deeply interrelated questions are particularly relevant for contemporary debate. The first relates to Kant's rationale for preferring a federation over a world republic, which includes the question concerning the powers of this supranational institution. The second concerns the criteria by which states qualify to enter the federation. Are only republics qualified to enter, or is any kind of state permitted? Since the last four sections of this essay focus on the first problem, we can confine ourselves now to some considerations concerning the second.

Unfortunately, Kant does not clearly indicate the membership criteria of his federation. We are thus left with the task of reconstructing his view from bits of textual evidence and, perhaps more importantly, systematic considerations that measure how well each of the two competing hypotheses squares with the general picture offered by Kant. Depending on the answer, we will attribute to Kant a model similar either to the European Union (EU) or to the United Nations (UN), just to mention the two most obvious examples, thereby shaping the normative indication of the second definitive article in profoundly different manners. In the first scenario, similar to that of the EU, Kant is suggesting a clear division of the world into two main zones: one that includes the already righteous states, and another that encompasses all the others. This is obviously the picture that Rawls assumes in *The Law of Peoples*, with one significant variation; namely that the club generously opens up its doors not only to liberal peoples, but also to the good enough, the "decent" ones. In the second scenario, more like that of the UN, the federation is a heterogeneous institution, where different kinds of regimes can meet and have permanent channels of diplomatic communication.

The key text in favor of the restricted reading, at times defended by careful interpreters such as Norberto Bobbio (Bobbio 2005, xiv), is probably the very title of the second definitive article.[18] There, Kant talks of a "federalism of *free states*" (ZeF 8:354; my emphasis). Since republics are the only "free" states, one would think that Kant is giving a rather clear indication, but this is not case. Indeed, "free" can also mean "independent" or "sovereign," or "not being under the command of anyone." As aptly pointed out by Eberl and Niesen, this is precisely the way in which Achenwall conceives of a "free" state (Eberl and Niesen 2011: 247). By characterizing potential members of the federation as "free states," Kant is better understood as emphasizing that they have surged to the level of full recognition in the international arena and/or that they are

---

[18] Although Bobbio seems to take the restricted reading for granted, he does provide an indirect reason for supporting it. He argues that the restricted access would explain why Kant feels confident that the lack of coercive powers on the part of the federation does not make it pointless: Since republics are pro-peace, they can reasonably be expected to externalize this attitude toward other republics without coercion. Obviously, if this were the case, the second definitive article would have scant, if any, force of its own: Its peace-promoting potential would seem to rest entirely on that of the first.

supposed to remain free – that is, independent – even if they join the federation.[19]

Moreover, Kant never explicitly restricts access to the federation to republican states. When he introduces the idea that if a people manages to form a republic, it can be "a focal point of federative union for other states" (ZeF:356) he does not say that these states must be republics. Of course, this is what he may have in mind, but the thought makes perfect sense even if one understands it in the sense that the new republic promotes and invites a federation with other states before their transition to the republican form, perhaps as a way of facilitating it. Moreover, in *The Contest of the Faculties* Kant argues that one should respect republics not only in "form" (i.e., representative, constitutional republics) but also in "mode," namely regimes in which those who hold power act "by analogy with the laws which a people would give itself in conformity with universal principles of right" (SF 7:88). The references to these *ante litteram* "decent peoples" indicate how Kant rejected a sharp division between virtuous and nonvirtuous states, which in turn counts as indirect evidence in favor of the open-access reading.

One systematic argument in favor of the open-access reading is that the alternative reading is committed to assigning to the federation the impoverished role of improving relations *between republics*. These relations should already be quite peaceful, given the logic of the first definitive article. To be sure, even inter-republican relations, as we know from history, are subject to controversies and tensions; in fact they have been quite frequent and still occur today. Hence, the permanent diplomatic channels ensured by the presence of a federation would still be of some use. Yet the role of the federation would be reduced to avoiding the comparatively rare cases in which republics find war between them useful and possible deontological dissuaders are not strong enough to halt the bellicose pursuit of their interests. This diminished role for the federation can hardly be compatible with the status Kant assigns to the second article, namely that of a definitive article as important as republicanism within states. Much more plausible is that the federation is thought of as providing those war-avoiding incentives when and where they are most needed; that is, in the relations between democracies and autocracies, and between autocracies. The presence of permanent diplomatic channels seems to be far more important in cases in which neither mutual trust nor mutual respect can be assumed.

---

[19] The restricted-access reading does not rest merely on this passage. Michael Doyle (2012) backs it up through a series of arguments crafted to respond to the protests of some Kant scholars, such as Cavallar (1999) and MacMillan (1995). I offered my reply to Doyle's points in Caranti (2017a: 143–6).

Over and above systematic considerations, Kant's own example of the federation was the assembly of Dutch States General at the Hague in the first half of the eighteenth century: "ministers of most of the courts of Europe and even of the smallest republics lodged with it their complaints about attacks being made on one of them by another" (MS 6:350). Kant also says that "each neighboring state is at liberty to join" the "association" or "permanent congress of states" (MS 6:350). Finally, he insists that these ministers promisingly thought of Europe as a single confederated state, "which they accepted as an arbiter in all their public disputes." Clearly this is the example of a mixed federation, not that of a club of republics, a club that at the time Kant is referring to would have probably included only the Swiss cantons (and not all of them) and later, at the time Kant was writing, only the Swiss cantons themselves, the French Republic, and perhaps the United States (depending on whether the fact that slavery was allowed in most states counts as a sufficient reason to disqualify the latter as a republic).

That is not all. In the paragraph that follows the example of the assembly of Dutch States General, Kant describes the federation as a "rational idea of a peaceful, even if not friendly, thoroughgoing community of all nations on the earth that can come into relations affecting one another" (MS 6:352). Here, the only membership criterion is the ability of peoples to enter into active relations with one another (thereby creating the risk of conflict and the corresponding war-averting institutional response), not the justice of their internal institutions. Combined with Kant's idea that all peoples (already in his times) were in a condition to affect one another (ZeF 8:360), this indicates quite clearly that Kant was thinking of a federation which nonrepublican states could and should enter. Now the question becomes: any non-republican state? Well, there seem to remain two categories of states that even on the open-access reading could not be accepted into the Federation. On the one hand, Kant describes as an "unjust enemy" the state "whose publicly expressed will (whether by word or deed) reveals a maxim by which, if it were made a universal rule, any condition of peace among nations would be impossible" (MS 6:349). These are not only despotic states, but also ones that are aggressive toward other sovereign entities. The obvious question arises of what sense it would make to open the doors of a league for peace to states that publicly announce a violent manner of conducting their external affairs. On the other hand, Kant also has the notion of barbaric states, which, as we discover in the *Anthropology*, are characterized by force without law and freedom. It is not the compression of freedom that disqualifies them (this happens in "merely" despotic states). Unlike the case of "unjust enemies," what causes the problem is not their external behavior. Rather it is the absence of the rule of law that disqualifies them. In order to sign a treaty (including the statute of the league) a state needs to prove that it is not ruled by the mere caprice of those who hold power but by laws that cannot be changed at will. Still, nonaggressive despotic states governed by the rule of law would be able to join. On the open-access reading, it would be even more important to have them rather than republics inside the federation because of their comparatively higher degree of bellicosity (ex first definitive article) and because membership in a peaceful federation would diminish the appeal of strong and nonaccountable executives to defend the country, thereby facilitating the transition toward republicanism.

This brings us to the final point. If the federation is thought of as encompassing any willing state, its role squares much better with the logic of gradual progress toward peace that seems to pervade Kant's project. The inclusion of as many existing states as possible seems to parallel Kant's point in the third definitive article in which economic and cultural interdependence is thought of as a peace-inducing factor that should affect all kinds of states, not just the relations between republics.

2.4 The Third Definitive Article

Kant complements his "recipe for peace" with a recommendation – one which is, as we shall see, quite novel in his political thinking – that concerns what he calls cosmopolitan right (*Weltbürgerrecht*). We read that "Cosmopolitan right shall be limited to conditions of universal hospitality," which is to be understood as a "*right to visit;* this right, to present oneself for society, belongs to all human beings by virtue of the right of possession in common of the earth's surface" (ZeF 8:358). He also claims that cosmopolitan right is a "supplement to the unwritten code of state right and international right necessary for the sake of any public rights of human beings and so for perpetual peace" (ZeF 8:360). Not only is cosmopolitan right now clearly distinguished from the other two branches of rights, but Kant also makes clear that without the right to visit, the other two branches, indeed all rights of human beings, are in danger. The relation of interdependence between public and international rights that Kant had emphasized in the seventh thesis of *Idea* is here reaffirmed and expanded to include a new branch of rights – the cosmopolitan one – which Kant had still not clearly distinguished in 1784. Without the global recognition of the right to visit, perpetual peace will never be reached. But what exactly is cosmopolitan right's contribution to peace? How does it make it more likely?

There are two main ways – one narrow, one broad – to read the causal link between the right to visit and peace. On the one hand, one can narrowly see the right to visit as a condition that enables economic interdependence, considered as the true peace-promoting factor. On the other hand, one may recognize this enabling function but read more than this into the right to visit. Among Kant specialists, the narrow reading has some acceptance. Allen D. Rosen (1993) and Samuel Fleischacker (1996), for example, construe Kant as a somewhat naïve free trade supporter. On their reading, Kant's cosmopolitan right would simply secure a prerequisite of international trade, by guaranteeing that individuals are permitted to move across frontiers. Kevin Thompson (2008) thinks that the "commerce [*Verkehr*]" between peoples Kant secures through cosmopolitan right is exclusively economic commerce (*contra* Kleingeld 2012: 75). Recently Massimo Mori has argued that cosmopolitan right is probably to be understood even more narrowly: It is a right of travelers not to be violently attacked if they set foot on foreign land, which is less than a right to visit that land (Mori 2008: 144–6).[20] Byrd and Hruschka (2010: 207–11) reaffirmed the narrow reading, suggesting that in the *Metaphysics of Morals* Kant conceptualizes cosmopolitan law in terms of the idea of a perfect World Trade Organization.[21] But it is mainly outside the circle of professional Kant scholars that the narrow reading has become popular, especially among democratic peace scholars. Kant's third ingredient for peace is reduced to economic interdependence.[22]

What about the alternative, broad reading? It is probably safe to say that most Kant scholars favor this interpretation, whose central idea is that cosmopolitan right is something more than international trade (or a way of securing it). For example, Ripstein realizes that the right to visit is about opening up frontiers to foreigners by virtue of the "disjunctive possession of the Earth's surface" (Ripstein 2009: 296), and commerce is only one of the many relations individuals have a right to propose to inhabitants of receiving countries. Ruyssen (1924: 355–71), Kersting (1996: 172–212) and Marini (2001: 19–34) see cosmopolitan right as the constitutional law of a world state. Waldron (2000) interprets Kant's cosmopolitan right mainly as the disposition not to take our conceptions of justice as nonnegotiable in dealing with people and peoples with

---

[20] Mori also argues that cosmopolitan right has a limited significance in the economy of Kant's model because it aspires to be a right (not philanthropy) and yet has no institutional backing. Basically, it is left to the goodwill of rulers to respect foreigners' right to visit, but no supranational force or authority is foreseen in case of violations (Mori 2008: 147–8).

[21] Cosmopolitan law would be nothing but "an ordered *iustitia commutativa* on the international level in the absence of a *iustitia tutatrix* and a *iustitia distributiva* in a state of nation states" (Byrd and Hruschka 2010: 211).

[22] For example, in a passage from the 1983 "Kant, Liberal Legacy, and Foreign Affairs," we read: "[t]he cosmopolitan right to hospitality permits the 'spirit of commerce' sooner or later to take hold of every nation, thus impelling states to promote peace and to try to avert war" (Doyle 1983a: 231). In other words, the whole point of cosmopolitan right is to promote trade, which in turn promotes peace. Notice also that Doyle inverts the causal order. While the "spirit of commerce" is in Kant explicitly presented as the means by which cosmopolitan right is expected to obtain recognition worldwide, in Doyle it becomes the end secured by cosmopolitan right.

different views. Taraborelli argues that the right to visit is a right that "guarantees everyone's opportunity to become 'associated' with a new nation and possibly, in some future time, to become a fellow inhabitant" (Taraborelli 2006: 153). Brown (2009) sees a commitment to a global morality (albeit of minimal reach). Eberl and Niesen argues that cosmopolitan right is essentially a "right to communication" (Eberl and Niesen 2011: 251). Similarly, Kleingeld construes cosmopolitan right as a right – ultimately springing from humans' innate right to freedom (MS: 236) – to attempt to initiate all sorts of communicative exchange, including, but not limited to, commercial interactions (Kleingeld 2012: 83–4).[23] Also Cavallar stresses that the interactions guaranteed by cosmopolitan right are not exclusively commercial ones (Cavallar 2002: 360). Although his recent book attacks the idea that Kant can be considered a cosmopolitan all the way through, Cavallar still characterizes Kant's position as a form of "thin moral cosmopolitanism" (Cavallar 2015: 2), which is already more than what the narrow reading is ready to concede. A yet broader reading was suggested by Anderson-Gold (2006), who pointed out that cosmopolitan right is not only a negative right, about refraining from hostilities against foreigners, but a positive right to a "dynamic interactive community of moral interdependence that is the only condition under which states could consistently adhere to international laws that are also universally just" (Anderson-Gold 2006: 138). Consonant with this approach is Derrida's famous account of hospitality as, among other things, a condition for epistemic progress thanks to the different perspectives that *l'étranger* brings into the receiving community (Derrida 2000). From this perspective, cosmopolitan right is about the creation of a global community in which various moral traditions search for and find common ground. This common normative commitment is the sole guarantee that sovereign states, in the absence of a world government, will stick to any legal obligations that they may be subject to in international institutions.

Thus far the representatives of the narrow and of the broad reading. Which reading should one prefer? There is little doubt that the idea that economic interdependence is good for peace is part of what lies behind the third definitive article. Kant says that nature "unites nations" and that it "does so by means of their mutual self-interest. It is the spirit of commerce, which cannot coexist with war and which sooner or later takes hold of every nation" (ZeF 8:368). There is no indication, however, that the significance of the article is limited to the

---

[23] Kleingeld (2012: 136–7) mentions Hegewisch as a naïve believer in the quick and easy equation between trade and peace in order to highlight the distance between Hegewisch's views and Kant's. She also criticizes Rosen (1993: 74, 76, 211) and Fleischacker (1996: 385) for downplaying Kant's cosmopolitanism in favor of Adam Smith's view that free international trade and the market are intrinsic values as well as peace-promoting factors.

peace–trade nexus. In fact, this is not even the core of the article. To begin with, the "spirit of commerce" appears only in the section devoted to the guarantee of perpetual peace, where Kant offers us reasons to believe that nature promotes the realization of each of the three branches of right. Regarding the third branch, it is the "spirit of commerce" – a natural drive – that shows how nature "pushes" for cosmopolitan right. In other words, the "spirit of commerce" is the instrument provided by nature for the realization of the end, that is, cosmopolitan right. Why conflate means and end when Kant so clearly distinguishes between them?

Furthermore, in the attempt to expand and clarify cosmopolitan right Kant talks about a right that one has "to present onself for society." Kant seems to have in mind a right to apply to enter a new social compound that he at times calls "a society" – as in this passage – but more often, and quite significantly, a "community."[24] Clearly, we are dealing here with something more than the sheer right to cross frontiers to do business in a foreign country. Rather, we have a right that is thought of as a means through which we can get to know each other, and come into contact with foreigners in order to lay down the basis of a community wider than the national one. In this sense, the third article pertains to *cosmopolitan* right. It focuses on the conditions that prevent peoples' reciprocal closure. It enables us to engage in those "good practices" that are needed to make sure that societies influence one another, know one another, and thus decrease the level of reciprocal distrust.

Still, in the versions of the broad reading discussed above, the impression is that at least one crucial aspect remains insufficiently highlighted, perhaps even in the particularly broad reading of Anderson-Gold (2006). This concerns the relation between cosmopolitan right and a global moral community. In a famous passage Kant claims that such a common conscience exists and is growing stronger among human beings. The reason why cosmopolitan right is not "fantastic and exaggerated" (ZeF 8:360) – he says – is that "the (narrower or wider) community of the nations of the earth has now gone so far that a violation of right on *one* place of the earth is felt in *all*" (ZeF 8:360). In other words, there is a universal community with a common moral conscience that condemns violations of human beings' natural rights. Precisely that common conscience is the guarantee that cosmopolitan right is not a mere utopian ideal. Moreover, the fact that the amount of respect for human beings dictated by that moral conscience is translated into an article of law is destined to strengthen and further develop the same moral conscience. Given its very content – the right to

---

[24] In the *Metaphysics of Morals* Kant says that cosmopolitan right grants humans a right "to *visit* all regions of the earth" while they "*try to* establish a community with all" (MS 6:353).

cross frontiers securely – cosmopolitan right enables and promotes mutual knowledge and various dimensions of interdependence (economic, cultural, demographic) which reinforce and gradually expand that global moral conscience, taking it beyond the normative basis underpinning the recognition of a universal right to visit. Indeed, as Kant himself says, although this natural right of hospitality does not extend beyond the conditions that make it possible to *attempt* to enter into relations with the native inhabitants, it nonetheless bridges distant continents and opens up otherwise closed nations, thus bringing the human race "ever closer to a cosmopolitan constitution [*weltbürgelichen Verfassung*]" (ZeF 8:358).[25]

3 The Project of Perpetual Peace in the Context of the Critical Philosophy

The three definitive articles unequivocally constitute the backbone of Kant's project. This does not mean, however, that they can be read in isolation – as they often have been. They are obviously embedded in a broader philosophical project constituted by Kant's critical philosophy as a whole. To begin with, Kant's model evidently rests on his teleological view of human affairs. One aspect of this view, or perhaps I should say the most extreme (hence clearest) part of that view, is the famous thesis according to which nature provides a "guarantee" that humanity will one day reach perpetual peace. It is fair to say that it is this thesis that has caused most problems of compatibility between Kant's peace project and his overall philosophy to be noticed. Another point of tension is undoubtedly the relation (or apparent disagreement, as Kant says) between politics and morality. Without passing over the extent to which some tension remains, I am going to suggest that no real incompatibility occurs in either of the cases.

3.1 The Guarantee Thesis

In his political writings Kant often claims that the achievement of a condition of perpetual peace among nations is guaranteed by nature. In one form or another, this thought recurs from *Idea for a Universal History with a Cosmopolitan Purpose* (1784) to the late *The Contest of the Faculties* (1798). Perhaps the

---

[25] For a criticism of my broad reading see Guyer (2019: 286–7). Guyer fears that expanding the significance and content of cosmopolitan right over and above the sheer right to visit risks obscuring Kant's anticolonialist intent. I believe, however, that highlighting how the right to visit on the one hand rests on the existence of a global conscience and on the other hand promises to further expand it, in turn thereby generating the necessary moral preconditions for an enhanced cultural and economic interdependence among peoples vindicates instead of betraying the anticolonialist significance that Kant attached to this branch of right.

clearest, strongest, and therefore most controversial version of this thought is to be found in *Toward Perpetual Peace* (1795) where Kant writes:

> What affords this *guarantee* (surety) is nothing less than the great artist *nature (natura daedala rerum)* from whose mechanical course purposiveness shines forth visibly, letting concord arise by means of the discord between human beings even against their will (ZeF 8:360–1).

How exactly does nature bring us perpetual peace to humans despite their discord, or better, by using it? To begin with, nature exploits humans' aggressive tendency to spread them to all areas of the world, "even into the most inhospitable" (ZeF 8:363). In addition, "it makes use of two means to prevent peoples from intermingling and to separate them: differences of *language* and of *religion*" (ZeF 8:367). These differences potentially cause hatred and violence, but they also prevent humanity from falling into a universal, colorless despotism deprived of pluralism and healthy competition among nations. Finally, nature – continues Kant – uses her most acute trick to ensure that differences remain but do not degenerate into permanent conflict. She exploits humans' greed and uses "the *spirit of commerce*, which cannot coexist with war and which sooner or later takes hold of every nation" (ZeF 8:368). If humans want to follow their greedy plans, they have to learn to live in a competitive yet peaceful global society. Thus Kant concludes:

> In this way nature guarantees perpetual peace through the mechanism of human inclinations itself, with an assurance that is admittedly not adequate for predicting its future (theoretically) but that is still enough for practical purposes and makes it a duty to work toward this (not merely chimerical) end.
> (ZeF 8:368)

Many have read this prediction as nothing but an example of simpleminded faith in progress, typical of the Enlightenment, and even sympathetic interpreters have judged it to be incompatible not only with contemporary epistemology but also with Kant's own fundamental theoretical and moral principles (Guyer 2006; Ludwig 2006). Howard Williams argued that even if we take Kant's optimism, as he calls it, not as an empirical claim, but as a normative suggestion inspired from reflective judgment on the intended direction of history and mainly directed toward moral politicians, his stance may still prove counterproductive and dangerous because it tends to generate victims in certain circumstances (Williams 1992). In general, one can distinguish three different arguments that challenge Kant's thesis at the epistemological, anthropological, and moral levels.

One way to express the epistemological concern is to say that predicting that a perpetual, that is, nonreversible peace will take place comes problematically close to the inferences of the mathematical antinomies before Kant's critical cure. There, it will be recalled, the illegitimate attempt was that of embracing the totality of experience. In the present case, one assumes a complete knowledge of all historical events, as required by the idea of a "final goal of history" and even more so by the idea of nonreversibility. Perhaps more importantly, leaving the problem of compatibility aside, one may legitimately wonder precisely what empirical or theoretical reasons Kant has to be so confident that perpetual peace is the goal toward which humanity – willingly or unwillingly – tends (Guyer 2006: 162–5).

The anthropological concern argues that if man is radically evil in the sense of having a disposition to prioritize self-love over morality, as Kant claims in *Religion Within the Limits of Reason Alone*, even assuming that there is a plan of nature favorable to peace, how can there be a guarantee that this plan is not subverted by humans' propensity for evil (Guyer 2006: 166–8)? Finally, the moral concern starts from the observation that if nature does the job of bringing about peace *despite us*, then the *duty* to promote perpetual peace risks becoming void. People cannot be obliged to do what is beyond their capabilities, but they cannot be obliged to bring about a state that is inevitable anyway either (Ludwig 2006: 185).

In a previous publication I offered a response to each of these concerns (Caranti 2014). To cut a long story short, I replied to the epistemological argument in two steps. First, I suggested that among the various versions of the thesis one can read in Kant's texts one should select and focus on the relatively weak claim that there are "good grounds" for believing that we shall succeed in bringing about a condition of peace, "albeit by an infinite process of gradual approximation" (ZeF 8:386). This is sufficient to establish the meaningfulness of our duty to realize a condition of public right (at the domestic, the international, and the cosmopolitan levels), but it is still compatible with the possibility that that final goal will be reached only through an asymptotic approximation. Second, I suggested that the "good grounds" are to be understood as basic, general empirical claims, for which no explicit argument is given, probably because Kant takes them as self-evident: (1) human nature is stable enough to allow some generalizations, for example that all humans strive toward happiness and the fulfillment of the material conditions that make happiness possible; (2) these material conditions can be met through means other than the instrument of war, for example through trade in conditions of peace; (3) humans can learn about the costs of the instrument of war and the benefits of these alternative means; (4) the residual obstacles to the adoption of these better means, such as uncertainty about the intentions of other players in the anarchical system of international affairs, can be removed through feasible reforms of the international order.[26] If (1)–(4) are true, it does seem to follow that the "system" of human affairs tends toward one determined end. The main idea is that humans are simply asked to realize that much, if not all that they expect from war can be attained through different, better means. All this licenses the belief that there is an *objective tendency* toward a peaceful outcome or, which I take as equivalent, that there is an objective probability that human affairs will evolve toward that outcome. There may be strictly speaking no *guarantee* that perpetual peace will ever be reached, but there is a guarantee that the world, at least the world as we know it now, is objectively "biased" in favor of an infinite approximation toward that outcome. So construed, the argument is certainly not free of difficulties, because it still depends on the truth of some other basic facts Kant probably did not even consider (for example that the resources of our planet will always be sufficient to satisfy the basic needs of all human beings, only provided that they live in just institutions), but it is at least made more in line with the limits that Kant sets to our knowledge (no straightforward ambition to embrace the totality of appearances) and is certainly not grounded on blind, simpleminded optimism. Moreover, so understood, the thesis is sufficient for us to make sense of our efforts in favor of peace and to remain immune from the demotivating rhetoric of moralizing politicians. Finally, the thesis' theoretical ambition is vindicated. We are not asked to endorse an article of faith only to make our moral agency meaningful. We have some objective grounds to believe that the world will approximate a condition of peace.

In response to the moral concern – how there can be a duty to bring about a condition that, it is stipulate, will happen anyway, I relied on the idea that Kant often presents (IaG 8:27; TP 8:310) of *accelerating* through our actions the coming of the period of peace which would supposedly come anyway thanks to the work of nature/providence. Even if perpetual peace will happen anyway (or better, even if it is constantly, albeit not linearly, approximated), there is still a duty on our part to realize those institutional reforms that will speed up the process (and the obvious symmetrical prohibition to abstain from behavior that will decelerate it). After all, Kant's view of progress always has a subjective and an objective component. The objective component is the natural/providential mechanisms that push us toward perpetual peace regardless of whether we embrace our duty to do what is in our power to bring about this condition. The subjective component is our moral resolution to do what is in our power to introduce those reforms that would crystallize progress in institutional forms,

---

[26] In other words, the obstacles are just a question of coordination among agents, as opposed to insuperable blocks inherent to human nature.

with roles and responsibility that vary depending on whether we are heads of state, intellectuals, or ordinary human beings.

In reply to the anthropological concern – that if humans are radically free and in particular radically evil, they can always deviate from the course that nature designs for the achievement of what morality wants – I argued that it borders inconsistency. The criticism does not challenge the assumption that the interests of individuals and groups are better served by peace than war (in our example, enrichment through peaceful commercial relations). Moreover, it stipulates that the radically evil person deviates from morality out of self-love. Now, the obvious question is why they should subvert a course of nature that *in the long run* promises to promote their own self-love.

In a recent counter-reply, Guyer argues that I make things too easy. On the one hand, he writes, "for Kant self-love subsumes all 'material' grounds for choice (see Critique of Practical Reason, Theorem II, 5: 22), thus the desire to gratify any sort of inclination, even the most momentary inclination to pervert what would otherwise seem to be the moral destination of nature just for the fun of it" (Guyer 2019: 285). I take this to mean that the radically evil person is always at liberty to prioritize the satisfaction of a whim over what is necessary to further the moral destination of nature, perhaps even if this is against their best interest. Moreover, Guyer continues, I problematically assume that "all human beings, or at least any in a position of power sufficient to influence the larger course of human affairs, have a sound, prudentially rational grasp of the long-term consequences of their actions" (Guyer 2019: 285). This assumption, however, is hardly compatible with the very common experience of foolish leaders that cannot even calculate their own long-term self-interest or the interest of the people they represent. In fact, continues Guyer, they cannot be expected to be able to do so, because one of Kant's central moral tenets is that humans are not very good at identifying the means to their happiness, and are therefore equally unable to see what is in their personal and/or collective self-interest (GMS 4:418–19).

Guyer is certainly right about these two points, but it is not true that I did not consider them, at least to a certain extent. In my original argument, concerning the well-known cases of foolish leadership, I conceded that "Kant's mechanisms may be insufficient to ensure that the particular interests of a few people do not trump the general good" (Caranti 2017a: 231). This is clearly different than raising the possibility of poor calculators, because I was focusing on particular/private (presumably well-calculated) interests trumping the interest of humanity at large. And yet, the solution I offered to my own concern applies also to Guyer's. I said that particular interests may *at times* trump the general interest (which by definition is considered to be compatible with peace). But if there is a natural objective propensity in favor of peace *and* this is in line with the best interest of people, then these perverse cases are *in the long run* destined to become more and more rare. To recalibrate a metaphor that I used in my argument, if the world system is rigged in favor of perpetual peace like a die is rigged in favor of outcome, say, "6," it is very possible that "6" will not always be the outcome, but "6" in the long run will obviously be the most frequent result. Moreover, if we believe that humans can learn, the bias toward perpetual peace, unlike that in favor of "6," will become heavier and heavier as time goes by. Hence even if human beings, and political leaders in particular, are unable to see now what is in their best interest, it still follows that experience will teach them that peace, not war, best serves their interests, even if the latter are fully immune to moral scrutiny.

This also speaks to Guyer's general point, which would make my reading "un-Kantian," that for Kant humans are no good at calculating what makes them happy. True, but only up to a point. We may be bad at knowing what makes us happy, but Kant clearly assumes that we know what makes us unhappy. If he did not, not only would his entire argument about learning from past atrocities collapse, but also his very idea of a juridical condition emerging even out of a race of devils would have the same destiny. In sum, I do not deny at all, as Guyer thinks, that radical evil can decelerate the progress. I never assumed Kant had a linear process in mind. But I do deny that these decelerating events are sufficient to conclude that there is no guarantee of perpetual peace, if by that we mean the weak claim recalled above, namely that the world has a propensity (an objective likelihood) in favor of peace. And I affirm that, contrary to appearances, it makes sense to construe an objective propensity as a form of guarantee of the final result (perpetual peace), if that objective propensity is thought of as influencing human affairs over an unlimited course of time.

3.2 Knowledge, Morality, and Politics: The Role of the Moral Politician

If the first supplement devoted to the guarantee thesis clarifies how Kant sees his project as destined to unfold in time through objective mechanisms, the first part of the appendix deals with the complementary and equally important component of individual initiative. What can single individuals do to further (or hinder) progress toward perpetual peace? Kant discusses here a number of ideal characters, from the moral politician to the political moralist, the moralizing politician, and the despotizing moralist. Together they constitute his theory of the good (and bad) political action. While the moral politician advances the cause of peace, the other figures are either ineffective or counterproductive, either because of unenlightened zeal (the despotizing moralist) or because of a mistaken perception of the hierarchy between morality and politics (the political moralist), or because of a self-fulfilling skepticism about what can be expected of human beings (the moralizing politician). By looking at these characters one can understand the manner in which Kant conceives of the relationship between the different parts of his moral philosophy broadly understood to encompass right, ethics, and politics. One can hardly place the project of perpetual peace in the context of the critical philosophy without paying attention to this point.

The first section of the appendix is entitled "On the Disagreement Between Morality and Politics in Relation to Perpetual Peace." Kant defines politics as a "doctrine of right put into practice [*ausübende Rechtslehre*]" (ZeF 8:370) and morality as a "theoretical branch of right [*theoretische Rechtslehre*]" (ZeF 8:370). By morality, whose alleged disagreement with politics is the subject of the entire section, Kant means here the system of juridical (not ethical) duties, in turn articulated in public, international, and cosmopolitan right. Politics is the application of these principles to reality. While right prescribes what ought to be done with no regard for the consequences, in particular with no regard to the context in which the rightful action would fall, politics is all about defining a wise, hence effective, application of the juridical principles to a specific reality. Politics is thus subordinated to right, which offers the general normative framework that guides political action, and yet it is partially independent of it because it must find for itself, that is, with no help from right, the most effective means to advance the principles of right. Kant attacks the position of those (realists, cynics, opportunists) who claim that real life has its own logic and does not/cannot follow the precepts of right, but at the same time recognizes that politics has nothing to do with a blind application of the juridical principles to the specific reality before us. The maxims of politics and morality are different, respectively "*Be ye therefore wise as serpents*" and "*guileless as doves*" (ZeF 8:370), and Kant does not suggest abandoning the first to let the second triumph. The prudence/expediency of politics must not be canceled out by the innocence of morality. The idea is rather that politicians must be "wise as serpents," but at the service of morality. Indeed, Kant defines the moral politician as the one who "conceives of the principles of political expediency in such a way that they can coexist with morality" (ZeF 8:372).

As already noted, Kant distinguishes the moral politician from three negative characters: the political moralist, the despotizing moralist, and the moralizing politician. They all misconceive the relation between morality and politics and for this reason hinder, or at least do not further, the cause of peace. The political moralist is one "who frames a morals to suit the statesman's advantage" (ZeF

8:372, my emphasis). Notice how the reference to his advantage *as a stateman* suggests that he is not necessarily a self-interested opportunist. He may be someone who– in good faith – thinks that it is *right* that morality be at the service of *raison d'état*. Morality may and should be reinterpreted if this operation is carried out by the (responsible) statesman. We are thus far from the case of those who surreptitiously gloss over "political principles contrary to right on the pretext that human nature is not capable of what is good in accord with that idea, as reason prescribes it" (ZeF 8:373). These are the "moralizing politicians," who are much more harmful than political moralists because they "make improvement impossible, and perpetuate, as far as they can, violations of right" (ZeF 8:373). Moralizing politicians are also more damaging than despotizing moralists. The latter merely "offend in various ways against political prudence (by measures prematurely adopted or recommended)" (ZeF 8:373), and yet by so doing they give themselves the chance to learn from the experience of their mistakes.[27]

There is also an interesting and controversial dimension to this discussion of the various ideal types of politician. It concerns the relation between political initiative and knowledge. Kant's official line of thought, expressed through the famous image of the conflict between the tutelary god of morality and Jupiter (ZeF 8:370), is that political moralists try to predict all the consequences of their moves to steer reality toward their goal. But reason is unable to provide certain and reliable indications about this: "reason is not sufficiently enlightened to survey the series of predetermining causes that would allow it to predict confidently the happy or unhappy results of human actions" (ZeF 8:370). In contrast, reason provides very clear indications about what it is morally mandatory to do: "it throws enough light everywhere for us to see what we have to do in order to remain on the path of duty (in accordance with rules of wisdom), and thereby do toward the final end" (ZeF 8:370). The suggested picture is thus that the political moralist attempts to steer the course of events by maneuvering the existing forces toward a desired outcome. In doing so, however, he is bound to failure because reason cannot predict with sufficient precision how events will unfold. In contrast, the moral politician only listens to pure practical reason to orient his action, does not need to have an accurate view on the unfolding of events, and therefore is not exposed to the failure of the political moralist.

---

[27] Regarding the despotizing moralists and their lack of prudence, remember the point we made in discussing the preliminary articles. There Kant clarified that three of these articles (2–4) are *leges lates* precisely because one should avoid a situation whereby "implementing the law prematurely counteract[s] its very purpose" (ZeF 8:347). Moreover, in a famous footnote attached to this discussion of the authorization to delay the realization of certain laws, Kant gives his most explicit exposition of this theory of *leges permissivae* (ZeF 8:348).

This picture, however, is in evident tension with what we just learned about the moral politician. If he must be wise, even as astute as a serpent, then it seems that he must have a fairly accurate if not complete grasp of the consequences of the actions he is contemplating. Our cognitive power cannot be unreliable when it serves the political moralist and yet reliable when it serves the moral politician. How, then, are we to understand Kant's ultimate view of the use the moral politician must make of his predictive capacity and of knowledge in general?

Let us recall that moral politicians correctly attend to the hierarchical relation between morality and politics. Far from being moral fanatics, though, they know that a forceful and premature "republicanization" of institutions is both contrary to right (the denial of the right to rebellion) and, most of the time, counterproductive. Good politicians must therefore be prudent in this sense. And perhaps in another: They must know well the reality in which they operate in order to introduce those reforms that the context is ready to accept. Their prudence, however, does not have to become the arrogance of those who believe themselves to be able to identify *all* relevant variables and manipulate them toward the desired goal (even if that goal is perpetual peace). Our reason is significantly below that standard. Hence, Kant seems to be saying, sometimes we are asked to introduce or merely propose reforms without a clear and complete foresight of the consequences of our initiative. This should not paralyze us. Even if we cannot prove beyond any reasonable doubt that such and such reforms will advance our goal, at times we have to support them anyway, as long as we know that they are inspired by right. Even less should we give a hearing to moralizing politicians who ridicule our reforms because they know how the world goes. Like us, moralizing politicians cannot predict the consequences of our reforms, and cannot exclude the possibility of progress.

In sum, moral politicians embody the subjective conditions that, by favoring peace through individual initiative, complement the set of objective conditions described by Kant in the first supplement. When Kant talks about moral politicians he has in mind heads of state, ministers, delegates, ambassadors, and so on. In short, professional politicians. And yet everything he says also applies to the way in which concerned citizens should orient their political action. In both cases, political actors can and must (actually must, hence can) find the ultimate guidance for their action in the principles of right. Far from applying those principles blindly and mechanically, moral politicians must be able to read the context in which they operate and be wise, astute and, if necessary, cunning to further their cause. They need to know a lot, they need to be prepared, but they must be ready to act even if theoretical reason is unable to predict all the consequences of their action. Any uneasiness caused by our limited powers of prediction can be partially lessened by the thought that our rightful initiative harmonizes with the objective tendency of human affairs to evolve toward perpetual peace, which was established in the first supplement. While this is obviously compatible with grand and very costly failures by even the most prudent moral politicians, it should never become a reason for inaction or for flirting with the self-fulfilling prophesies of the moralizing politicians who "perpetuate, as far as they can, violations of right" (ZeF 8:373).

This ends our introduction to Kant's project of perpetual peace and of its place within the broader system of the critical philosophy. Needless to say, I have not covered all the important aspects of the project but merely reconstructed the general picture and focused on some hermeneutical puzzles present in a project that only *appears* to be straightforward and simple. More details are available in existing commentaries, some of which have appeared in the last decade (Byrd and Hruschka 2010; Eberl and Niesen 2011). It is now time to focus on the Kantian federation. In particular, I turn now to the aspect of the entire project that has attracted the most scholarly attention. What kind of supranational institution does Kant ultimately recommend for the sake of peace? Why does he, as it seems, end up preferring a voluntary league over a more ambitious international institution, either in the form of a federation of states with coercive powers or in the form of a single world republic? Are the reasons he presents for this choice defensible? Do they reflect merely pragmatic considerations related to absence of good will, on the parts of single states, to give up their sovereignty? Or do they rather have a normative substratum? The first step toward an answer is probably to look at the way Kant changed his mind over the years regarding the nature and powers of the supranational institution.

4 The Evolution of Kant's Thought on International Right

Very few interpreters deny that Kant has some hesitations when it comes to designing the nature and powers of the supranational institution that should contribute to world peace, along with republican institutions within states and the right to visit, recognized by states, of every human being. Even sympathetic scholars, who believe that Kant never changed his mind and always consistently preferred the option of a federal state of states, recognize that he designed different models: the single world state, the federal state of states, and the league of nations or confederation (Byrd and Hruschka 2010: 196–205). They also acknowledge that at least in the *Doctrine of Right* Kant advocates a fourth model of a "permanent congress," which they themselves construe as even weaker than the league of nations, because while the latter rests on some multilateral treaty signed by member states, the former remains in a precontractual stage (Byrd and Hruschka 2010: 204–5).

In fact, the very idea that Kant does not change his mind over the years on the point at issue is hard to defend. Kant first suggests the necessity of a supranational institution for the sake of peace in *Idea for a Universal History with a Cosmopolitan Purpose* (1784). As noticed by Mori, even if the alternative between a federation and a world state is not formulated, the reasons behind Kant's oscillation are already present (Mori 2008: 107–8). Kant first stresses the analogy between the domestic and the international case in the move from the state of nature to the civil condition. The same unsocial sociability that forced individuals to enter the civil condition leads peoples and states to abandon a lawless state and to enter "a federation of nations, where every state, even the smallest, could expect its security and rights not from its own might, or its own juridical judgment, but only from this great federation of nations (*Foedus Amphictyonum*), from a united might and from the decision in accordance with laws of its united will" (IaG 8:24). The logic of the analogy and the reference to a "united might," and, even more forcefully, to a "united will," suggest that Kant has something more in mind than a voluntary and contingent defense alliance. And yet the reference to the *Foedus Amphictyonum* goes in the opposite direction, because this was merely an alliance of neighboring Greek *poleis* to protect and maintain a religious site. Elsewhere in the essay Kant describes the federation as a "large state body" (IaG 8: 28) and as a "perfect state constitution" (IaG 8: 27). Both descriptions again suggest something similar to a world state, and yet the reference to "a law of equilibrium" (IaG 8: 26) to regulate the essentially healthy hostility which prevails among states, as well as the characterization of the federation as a "cosmopolitan condition of public state security" (IaG 8:26), which is "not wholly without *dangers*" (IaG 8:26), indicate that Kant has no intention of overcoming the state of nature at the international level in perfect analogy with the domestic case, but merely intends to establish a security system based on bilateral or multilateral treaties signed by members that remain fully sovereign. The fact that this system is characterized as "cosmopolitan" should not be taken as evidence of an endorsement of something more ambitious than a tentatively permanent defense alliance. In 1784 Kant has not yet distinguished international from cosmopolitan right with full clarity (Caranti 2017b).[28] Indeed, at that time Kant does not have a notion of cosmopolitan right as a distinct and independent branch of right that has nothing to do with the federation. Indeed, in the Feyerabend lectures (1784), there is no mention at all of cosmopolitan right. Moreover, there Kant says that "the *jus gentium* is merely the possibility of

---

[28] This point is not to be conflated with the one defended by Cheneval (2002), according to which, in the 1780s, Kant still makes no clear distinction between *Völkerstaat* and *Völkerbund*.

a *Völkerbund*" (V-NR/Feyerabend 27: 1393).[29] Hence, characterizing the supranational institution as "cosmopolitan" does not necessarily mean that Kant is advocating something more ambitious than an international federation that encompasses *all* states. Obviously, the ambiguity regarding the very nature of the institution translates itself into an ambiguity in terms of the powers the institution is supposed to have. It is not clear whether Kant in 1784 is ready to concede at least a partial transfer of national sovereignty to a higher political authority for the sake of peace.

The 1793 essay "On the Common Saying" introduces for the first time a clear distinction between "*cosmopolitan constitution*" under a common sovereign and "a rightful condition of *federation* under a commonly agreed upon *right of nations*." Kant says that the latter is to be preferred, if the former proves itself even more dangerous to freedom than the status quo "for it may lead to the most fearful despotism" (TP 8: 310–11). The first hermeneutical problem here is to understand whether, as it is at times argued (e.g., Mori 2008: 109), Kant intends the cosmopolitan constitution as the solution dictated by theory and the federation as the one suggested by practice. If this is the case, Kant would be grossly incoherent because the general goal of the essay is precisely to show that what is true in theory (read: dictated by practical reason) can always be realized and should never be abandoned on the basis of "practical" considerations. However, there is no clear indication that the cosmopolitan constitution is the only option suggested by theory. Kant appears to be presenting the alternative – that is, the federation under international right – as more palatable to a single world state *and yet fully still consistent with what theory demands*. This suggests that what he has in mind is not merely a voluntary confederation, but a federation *with coercive powers*. Moreover, the fact that Kant describes the supranational institution dictated by theory as subject to "enforceable public laws to which each state must submit" is too thin to serve as evidence to conclude that he is talking about a world state. A federation with coercive powers established by multilateral treaties among states would still satisfy that definition. Not accidentally, in a Reflexion (8065) from the eighties Kant explicitly describes the alternative to the world state; that is, the federation as that institutional setting that guarantees "the freedom of each state *under a universal law*" (Refl 19: 600 my emphasis).[30]

---

[29] No reference to cosmopolitan right is present in the *Reflexionen* of volume 19 of the *Akademie Ausgabe*. Those notes are dated no later than 1789, with only a couple of exceptions. Thanks to Frederick Rauscher for these points.

[30] To be sure, being "under a universal law" does not immediately imply being under coercive powers. After all, duties of virtue are universal but do not allow coercive enforcement (thanks to Paul Guyer for noticing this). And yet, since we are talking about the freedom of states, it is

To be sure, in 1793, on the crucial point of what shape and powers the supranational institution required by theory is supposed to have, Kant does not seem to hold firm beliefs. The example of a solution that is true in theory is what "the theory of Abbé St Pierre or Rousseau" (TP 8: 313) proposed. Now, while Rousseau may have endorsed a European federal state, that is a federation with coercive powers, St Pierre, whose position Kant knew well, never dreamed of proposing either a world state or a federation with coercive powers. His "Grand Alliance" was nothing but a defensive league and his "European Assembly" nothing but a permanent seat for diplomatic intercourse, that is, a (con)federation *without coercive powers*.

But if the federation (with or without coercive powers) is not the solution merely dictated by practice, what does practice suggest then? The "practical" surrogate to the solution true in theory is not the federation under international right, but the status quo or the highly unstable *"balance of powers in Europe"* (TP 8:313). Far from betraying the general orientation of the essay, this position squares perfectly with it.

If up to "On the Common Saying" Kant remains noncommittal as to the exact form the supranational institution is to take, from *Toward Perpetual Peace* (1795) on, his preference for the federation over the world federal state is stated clearly. Moreover, the federation itself becomes unequivocally "light." In the 1795 essay, right after having introduced the second definitive article, Kant clarifies that what must be established is a *"league of peoples"* which need not be a "state of nations" (ZeF 8:354). And the reason for this preference – roughly, the fact that the very notion of one international state is inconsistent – comes close to a repudiation of his previous opening up to the possibility of a world state. In the *Metaphysics of Morals* (1797), Kant will end up denying any coercive power to it, while affirming the freedom of member states to leave the federation at will.

Things are not so simple, however. Within the same essay Kant keeps recognizing the world-state/state-of-nations option as the rational one, or, as he puts it, the one true *in thesi*: "In accordance with reason there is only one way that states in relation with one another can leave the lawless condition, which involves nothing but war; it is that, like individual human beings, they give up their savage (lawless) freedom, accommodate themselves to public coercive laws, and so form an (always growing) state of nations (civitas gentium) that would finally encompass all the nations of the earth" (ZeF 8:357) In other words, the rational way to prevent war is to endorse that international state

---

reasonable to understand Kant's claim as occupied with a general duty *of right*, that it is, for him, analytically related to coercion.

(*Völkerstaat*) which Kant had described a few lines before as intrinsically contradictory. Moreover, the reasons that lead Kant to abandon what is true *in thesi* to endorse what is possible *in hypothesi* are fascinating. Since states, according to their conception of international right, place limitations on what is right *in thesi* – that is, they veto any solution that includes their disappearance as independent and sovereign entities – "in place of the positive idea *of a world republic* only the *negative* surrogate of a *league* that averts war, endures, and always expands can hold back the stream of hostile inclination that shies away from right, though with constant danger of its breaking out" (ZeF 8:357). The surrogate of the league is the solution possible *in hypothesi* because states are what is "posited below" (literally, in Greek, *hypo-tithemi* means "to put below"): They are already given and with their legitimate interest in remaining in existence, constitute a formidable obstacle to what is right *in thesi*.

While in the 1793 essay Kant conceded the existence of difficulties but remained confident that what is right in theory must also be possible in practice, now the fact that something is right *in thesi* is no longer a sufficient guarantee regarding the possibility of its implementation and can be put aside because of the obstacles states "posit" on the way toward the world state. So this is a double shift: on the one hand, from a noncommitment as to the best institutional form to an open endorsement of the federation as the only possible solution. On the other hand, it is a shift from trust that what reason commands is certainly feasible, to just the opposite: Something may be true in theory but does not apply in practice. Finally, if in 1793 Kant still thought that the supranational institution, no matter whether in the form of a single world state or a federated state of nations, had to be endowed with coercive powers to enforce the common laws binding all members, he is now careful to clarify that *if* the federation has to have any power, this is not analogous to the power the civil state has over citizens: "This league does not look to acquiring any power of a state but only to preserving and securing the freedom of a state itself and of other states in league with it, but without there being any need for them to subject themselves to public laws and coercion under them (as people in a state of nature must do)" (ZeF 8:356). Finally, and this point is crucial, unlike the world state, the federation may be feasible, but there is a price to pay. While the former guarantees that there will be no war, the latter merely makes war less likely (ZeF 8:357).

As anticipated, Kant's evolution toward a clear preference for the federation over the world state culminates in 1797's *Metaphysics of Morals*. Here Kant repeats that only a world state is capable of guaranteeing peace, by transforming international relations from a condition in which by necessity there can be only provisional right to a condition in which right becomes peremptory, in perfect analogy with the exit from the state of nature at the domestic level. And yet not only is the non-oercive nature of the federation reaffirmed ("the alliance must . . . involve no sovereign authority (as in a civil constitution)" (MS 6:344) but also its permanence in time is put at risk. While it remains true that, unlike a contingent gathering of states, the association is to be conceived as a "*permanent* congress of states," the federation "can be renounced at any time and so must be renewed from time to time." And to reinforce the point, Kant offers two further considerations. On the one hand, he indicates the 1719 Assembly of the States General at the Hague – a gathering of the major European powers ultimately leading to the 1720 Treaty of The Hague – as a good example of the federation as it should be understood.[31] On the other hand, he warns against conflating the federation with the United States of America, "which is based on a constitution and can therefore not be dissolved" (MS 6: 351).

If this is the evolution of Kant's position, it may be of interest to identify the models that Kant seems to have entertained and evaluated in this long and difficult journey. Byrd and Hruschka think there are three models, but I think that one can reasonably distinguish at least five, listed below in descending order of institutional ambition:

1. Single world state (TP 8:311), world republic (ZeF 8:357), or universal monarchy (ZeF 8:367). Transfer of states' sovereignty.
2. Federal state of states/nations (*Völkerstaat* or *allgemeiner Staatenverein*) TP 8: 312, 313; ZeF 8: 354, 357; MS 6: 311, 350. Transfer of states' sovereignty.
3. Federation with coercive powers (*Föderation*), different from the *Völkerstaat* because it is not a unified political body, does not have legislative authority on all areas, and yet there is a power (likely of judicial nature) issuing binding resolutions of controversies among members on the basis of the existing treaties, and possibly some form of executive power to execute sentences. (TP 8:311, Refl 19:600). Transfer of states' sovereignty on specific areas.
4. Federation without coercive powers or league (*Völkerbund* or equivalent expressions used by Kant such as *Friedensbund, Föderalität, freier Föderalism, föderative Vereinigung*), likely generated through international treaties with, so to speak, no expiration date, hence tentatively permanent. This is roughly equivalent with what we today call a mere confederation (ZeF 8:354, 356, 357). No transfer of states' sovereignty.

---

[31] A questionable example indeed, given that the Assembly was an ad hoc gathering meant to solve one crisis only (the war of the Quadruple Alliance) and was not intended to survive 1720. As such, it hardly had even the relative permanence – the "*permanent* congress of states" (MS 6:350) – Kant wanted.

5. "Permanent" congress of states (*Staatencongreß*), still in a precontractual stage, to be continuously renewed from time to time and dissoluble because members are allowed to pull out anytime (MS 6:350–1). No transfer of states' sovereignty.

Of course, the complexity increases if we distinguish between republican or despotic forms of the models that presuppose centralized coercive powers (models 1–3). There is also the crucial question of whether states can be coerced to participate in any of the models indicated above. On this very important point, Byrd and Hruschka are positive that for Kant states may be coerced (Byrd and Hruschka 2010: 194). They cite as evidence an indirect, which they call "formal" argument, and a more direct, explicit one. The first is that the postulate of public right, which introduces the general obligation to leave the state of nature and enter a civil condition, applies to all articulations of right. Indeed, in the *Doctrine of Right* Kant presents the postulate before he moves on to distinguish between the three juridical dimensions, and this suggests that it applies to all three of them. Interestingly, a similar point was made by a very early critic of Kant, Johann Gottlieb Fichte, who pointed to a footnote in *Toward Perpetual Peace* (ZeF 8:349) in which Kant has another version of the same postulate. Fichte, however, makes the point in order to reach the opposite conclusion; namely, that Kant is *not* faithful to his postulate because, when it comes to international relations, he is ready to make an exception. Fichte realizes that Kant wants (more or less consistently) the obligation for states to leave the state of nature to coexist with their freedom not to enter any supranational institution, especially if this has coercive powers and therefore promises to erode their sovereignty. And that this is the case is quite evident from what Kant says as early as 1795, when he describes the enlargement of the federation as starting with a powerful and enlightened people that establishes republican institutions and serves as a "focal point of federative union of other states, to attach themselves to it and so to secure a condition of freedom of states conformably with the idea of the right of nations; and by further alliances of this kind, it would extend further and further" (ZeF 8:356). Kant's language suggests a gradual and spontaneous process as opposed to one in which all states are simultaneously forced into the federation.

The second argument is that in paragraph 54 of the *Doctrine of Right* Kant says that states living in a state of nature are obliged to leave it (MS 6:344). But, of course, this does not seem to be enough evidence to conclude that Kant wants states to be coerced into respecting this obligation.[32] In fact, the opposite seems to

---

[32] The fact that for Kant the notion of right analytically implies that of coercion does not apply here. That analytic relation seems to be meant for the specific norms that hold within an already

be true. A few lines later, Kant indicates that the supranational institution which states are to enter is the league of nations that "can be renounced at any time and so must be renewed from time to time" (MS 6:344). Thus, on Byrd's and Hruschka's reading, Kant in this passage is saying that states can be coerced into entering an institution which they can leave at any time. This would be quite bizarre.

To sum up: Kant changed his mind over the years about the nature and powers of the supranational institution that he indicates as the second pillar of his model for peace. He leaned more and more toward a thin and loose league, which states have only a generic obligation to enter without being coerced to do so, and that they may dissolve at any time. However, Kant never changed his mind about the fact that the only guarantee of peace would be a world republic or a federation with coercive powers. This is obviously compatible with the idea that he ended up preferring, an institution that at best decreases the chances of war and that consequently needs the concurrence of the other two dimensions of right to deliver something approaching a guarantee of peace.

5 Three Lines of Argument in Favor of the Federation

Having reconstructed the evolution of Kant's position on the powers and nature of the supranational institution, the most fascinating and yet most difficult point still remains to be addressed. Why did he come to prefer the federation over the world state? Do his reasons stand up to scrutiny, or is the dissatisfaction expressed by many readers from very early on (Fichte) justified? Kant has profoundly different arguments to ground his preference, from empirical-pragmatic, to normative, to logical ones. Indeed one can distinguish three main lines of thought: (a) empirical-pragmatic arguments (a belief in the administrative inefficiency of a state covering too large a territory combined with its alleged tendency to move toward a soulless despotism and possibly a final stage of anarchy); (b) a logical argument (in the very idea of a state of states lies a contradiction, because a world state removes the very notion of *international* right); (c) a moral/juridical argument resting on the limits of the domestic analogy (states may not be forced to abandon the state of nature and enter a juridical condition because, unlike individuals in the state of nature, they already have a moral personality).

The first line of thought starts from an empirical claim concerning the past experience of an inverse relation between administrative efficiency and

---

established juridical condition. But here we are asking whether states can be coerced to create that very juridical condition, which is a different story. To be sure, states are still under the obligation to leave the state of nature but there is ample logical space in Kant's system to construe this obligation as a noncoercible one, such as, for example, the case of political leaders' obligation to reform domestic institutions to approximate republican standards.

extension of the territory over which a government rules: "as the range of government expands laws progressively lose their vigor" (ZeF 8:367). This is combined with another claim, no less empirical, regarding the necessary degeneration of such states. A "universal monarchy," but likewise also a state of states, would first degenerate into a "soulless despotism," probably in the desperate attempt to implement its rule over so large a territory. Alternatively, such a system would degenerate into anarchy, with the emergence of factions which the central authority had no sufficient power to keep in check. This is obviously not acceptable because anarchy is the state of nature which the supranational institution was meant to avoid. As Kant puts it, "if such a state made of nations were to extend too far over vast regions, governing it and so too protecting each of its members would finally have to become impossible" (MS 6:350). At times Kant does not make the last step in the argument from despotism to anarchy, because he takes as self-evident that even if a universal despotic government were capable of implementing its laws, they would still be the "graveyard of freedom" (ZeF 8:367), thereby guaranteeing peace at the cost of denying the supreme value (freedom) that all articulations of right (including the international one) are supposed to secure. In addition, and this may count as a further twist in this pragmatic line of thought, a world state would remove that healthy hostility among states which is necessary to prevent the powers of humanity "fall[ing] asleep" (IaG 8:26), and thereby hindering the cultural and moral improvement of the species.

As rightly noticed by Mori (Mori 2008: 117), no matter how sound these empirical claims are, they hardly harmonize with the general orientation of Kant's thought.[33] If a world state were "right in theory" one would not expect Kant to say that it is to be abandoned as a political goal only because experience suggests that it is difficult to realize in practice. The fact that large empires in the past have followed the path indicated by Kant could never be a sufficient reason for making what is right nonobligatory. As Kant himself puts it: "experience cannot teach what right is" (TP 8:306). And even more forcefully, what reason prescribes as right does not follow "from perceiving the ways of the world" and it remains obligatory "even though no example of this could be found" (MS 6:216). So any empirical argument meant to show either that the world state is

---

[33] Incidentally, the empirical claim loses its grip if we modify it from a concern about the size of the territory to one about the size of the population. Kant did not have the advantage of witnessing the case of Indian democracy. No one calls India an authoritarian state, and its rule extends over almost 1.4 billion people. From 1.4 billion to 7.5 billion (the world population) is not such a dramatic leap. If democracy or a republic can exist with a 1.4 billion population, there seems to be no principled reasons why it could not do so with a 7.5 billion population. Thanks to Alessandro Ferrara for this point.

too ambitious a political goal or inefficient/prone to degenerating should not be taken, at face value, as Kant's last word of the matter.

What about the second line of thought? The contradiction argument, presented in *Toward Perpetual Peace*, starts from the lawless condition of international relations and the obligation each state has to overcome it, by entering a league of nations. Kant is keen to clarify that this league

> need not be a state of nations. That would be a contradiction, inasmuch as every state involves the relation of a *superior* (legislating) to an *inferior* (obeying, namely the people); but a number of nations within one state would constitute only one nation, and this contradicts the presupposition (since here we have to consider the right of *nations* in relation to one another insofar as they comprise different states and are not to be fused into a single state).
>
> (ZeF 8:354)

Kant's reasoning is now that a world state, in establishing – like any other state – the relation between a superior and an inferior would end up denying the independence and sovereignty of states, thereby merging all of them into one. This would contradict the assumption that we are looking for an *international* institution, that is, something that preserves the plurality of juridical subjects signing the contract.

Three things are worth noticing. To begin with, notice Kant's language: "need not be a state of nations [*kein Völkerstaat sein müßte*]". If there is a contradiction in the very idea of a state of nations, then one would expect Kant to say something stronger to rule it out, like "may/should not be a state of nations." The fact is that, as I have said repeatedly, Kant never abandons the idea that the only true solution to the problem of war is precisely either the single world state or the federal state of states. And this emerges even when he is about to present an argument that supposedly spots a contradiction in that very idea.

Secondly, one could say that Kant does not consider the possibility of a *federal* state of nations, which allegedly would preserve the plurality of states while establishing a federal power above them. Obviously Kant does consider (and rule out) this possibility in the *Doctrine of Right*, when he clarifies that the league he wants should not be conflated with the United States of America. But by the light of the contradiction argument only, the impression is that Kant overlooks the possibility of a federal state that does not merge all states into one. This criticism is well grounded and yet – I believe – does nothing but reveal the ultimate reservation Kant seems to have toward anything more than a loose federation. This is the idea that if the federal state advocates competence for itself over the use of force against external actors, even if it leaves competence to states in other areas, then member states' sovereignty is completely lost. I will come back to this point because it constitutes the essence of my reading of Kant's preference for a league of states. For the moment, it is sufficient to notice that it is unlikely that Kant simply did not think of the federal option. He rather already considered it – albeit implicitly – incompatible with the sovereignty of the federated states.

Thirdly, even if this is correct, one may still ask Kant why we should preserve a plurality of states. What is it about nations that is so inviolable that it prevents us from imagining anything except a solution that overcomes them? Certainly, a world state would preclude the healthy competition among states that we saw in the pragmatic arguments, but this is too thin a basis. After all, much of the competition that stimulates human progress may happen between individuals, as we know from the domestic case. Even if the competition between peoples (or states) adds something to that between individuals, is the gain significant enough to give up the only institutional solution that would *guarantee* the permanent overcoming of war?

Alternatively, and more convincingly, one may try to boost Kant's argument by establishing a link between the existence of a plurality of states and the freedom of individual citizens living in those states. As we saw, Kant says that in a state a relation has already been established between a superior and an inferior. One way to understand this is that once a state is created, a rightful condition (more or less perfect depending on how institutions approximate the republican ideal) is also established. This juridical condition is the guarantee (again, more or less perfect) of the freedom of the consociates. They are part of a contract through which they had at least some of their rights and freedoms secured. A melting of all states into one, or even the erection of a federation with a central power and ultimate authority on possible disputes between federated states, would only be compatible with individual freedom if citizens freely renounced the juridical condition they had established in their domestic state and decided to enter a new juridical condition, this time at the global level.

Eberl and Niesen makes a similar point when they argue that a world state would violate the individual freedom of citizens already belonging to established domestic states, especially if the existing states in question were republics (Eberl and Niesen 2011: 240).[34] This, however, does not explain how Kant

---

[34] Also Kjartan Koch Mikalsen (Mikalsen 2019) proposes a Kantian argument in which national sovereignty is construed as a freedom-enabling institutional arrangement; that is, as an essential condition for the recognition of individuals as free and equal. The nerve of the argument seems to be that freedom requires, among other things, independence from others, understood as the liberty to construe one political community that is somehow *different from* other political communities. Hence it is not the institutional framework per se (a world government would secure that), but the institutional framework in which some individuals can be and be seen as different from other political communities.

can rule out through merely logical or normative arguments a world *republic*, where, at least in theory, individuals would have their sphere of freedom protected and secured just as well as they have it in domestic republics. I suggest that if one takes this question seriously then Kant's best argument, by no means conclusive and yet quite powerful, which rules out anything more than a loose federation as a viable option, becomes evident. What is key is to focus on the normative importance of states as "hypotheses," understood as what is already "posited below," as I explained in Section 4. The fact that states already exist is not a mere empirical accident that can be overcome by following blindly what reason commands and what peace requires (the world state or the federal state of states). Since states as "hypotheses" (ZeF 8:357) have already established a limited juridical condition in which a group of individuals has signed a pact empowering *that specific national commonwealth* to protect their freedom and inborn right(s), and to do it in one peculiar manner among the many possible, the burden to protect their freedom can be transferred to a higher, global institution only if the parties agree to annul the original contract and enter a new one. For sure, states cannot be *forced* to enter, because what reason commands at the international level cannot ignore what it commanded at the domestic level when the domestic juridical condition was created.

This introduces us to the third line of thought, which paves the way for Kant's most convincing case for the federation. The argument is based on the limits of the analogy between the domestic and the international case regarding the duty to abandon the state of nature:

> what holds in accordance with natural right for human beings in a lawless condition, "they ought to leave this condition," cannot hold for states in accordance with the right of nations (since, as states, they already have a rightful constitution internally and hence have outgrown the constraint of others to bring them under a more extended law-governed constitution in accordance with their concepts of right). (ZeF 8:355–6)

Kant evidently thinks that the fact that states have established a lawful condition "inside" makes their case different than that of individuals in the state of nature. While in the latter case there is still no trace of legality (at most there are innate natural rights of individuals to be protected through the rule of law), at the international level each commonwealth is already a legal entity, with a right to exercise its autonomy. As noticed by Mori (2008: 119–20), Kant expresses this conception of states' autonomy in the important Reflexion 8065 (Refl 19: 600) from the 1780s that we already cited, where the condition of individuals in the state of nature is likened to that of accidents in need of a substance (the civil constitution), while that of states is considered already a condition of substance.

A world state would downgrade substances to accidents. It follows that we have to discard the world-state option and adopt the federation, where each nation state keeps its sovereignty.

One important thing needs to be noticed. The legal autonomy already established internally does not remove the obligation to overcome a lawless condition in which each state is a constant threat to others. If there is an institutional setting that at the same time removes or mitigates that threat and maintains each state's autonomy, the state's obligation appears to be as strict as that of individuals. Even conceding that the analogy between the domestic and international case has limits, this at most removes the possibility for one state to *coerce* another to join a supranational institution under common laws, not the obligation for each state to do that *spontaneously*. Indeed, the autonomy of each state can never remove this obligation:

> Now morally practical reason pronounces in us its irresistible *veto: there is to be no war*, neither war between you and me in the state of nature nor war between us as states, which, although they are internally in a lawful condition, are still externally (in relation to one another) in a lawless condition; for war is not the way everyone should seek his right [*sein Recht*]. (MS 6:354)

6 Cosmopolitan Concerns: A Neglected Middle Term Between *Völkerstaat* and *Völkerbund*

Since the first appearance of *Toward Perpetual Peace*, many readers of Kant, including sympathetic ones, have been dissatisfied with his ultimate preference for a federation rather than the world republic or the federal republic of republics as a viable political option.[35] Particularly interesting is the position of moderate cosmopolitans who think that Kant could have endorsed a more ambitious solution without endangering the plurality and autonomy of states. Something along these lines animates four authoritative readings that have tried to show that, after 200 years of political experiments, we can aim higher than the mature Kant ultimately came to believe was possible. They probably constitute the best criticism of the federation available in the literature, and, more importantly, come close to the last-resort attempt to vindicate the possibility of

---

[35] In addition to the four scholars we are about to discuss, others who are either dissatisfied with Kant's preference for the federation without coercive powers or skeptical that he endorsed this solution as his favorite include the following: Axinn (1989), Bull (1977), Byrd and Hruschka (2010), Carson (1988), Friedrich (1948), Lutz-Bachmann (1997), Marini (1998), Nida-Rümelin (1996), and Wood (1995). In contrast, readings that support the *Völkerbund* either as Kant's ultimate preference or as the philosophically sound solution (or both) are the following: Brown (2005), Covell (1998), Doyle (1983a and 1983b), Ebbinghaus (1968), Gallie (1978), Gerhardt (1995), Hinsley (1963), Mulholland (1987), Philonenko (1988), Rawls (1999), Tesòn (1992).

a cosmopolitan solution to Kant's peace project. While in our opinion ultimately unsuccessful, they deserve attention because they reveal *a contrasto* the strength of Kant's arguments in favor of the federation.

Thomas Pogge (Pogge 2006) argues that Kant was blind to the possibility of something more ambitious than a loose federation because he was still operating with a modern conception of sovereignty, a conception based on the idea that sovereignty can only be absolute: undivided and unlimited. From Aquinas *via* Dante, Marsilius, Bodin, Hobbes, and Rousseau all the way to John Austin in the past century, the idea has always been that if sovereignty is limited, we have no sovereignty at all. Indeed, if a sovereign is to operate only within a limited mandate, who is to decide whether a certain decision legitimately falls within the scope of that mandate? We have only two possibilities. If the decision rests with the sovereign itself, then sovereignty is unlimited because the sovereign is the ultimate judge about the limits of its competence. If it is an external agency (imagine a supranational court), then the sovereign has *no* power because any exercise of its authority would depend on the supranational agency's acquiescence.

Pogge rebuts this classic manner of conceiving of sovereignty by noticing that in contemporary liberal democracies there is no institution within the system that exercises full sovereignty: Neither the parliament, nor the supreme court, nor any other institution has *ultimate* authority to decide possible conflicts of competences. This is even more evident – we might add – for the liberal democracies belonging to the EU, which not accidentally is considered by Pogge as a good example of the federation Kant should have endorsed. The sovereignty of member states is limited by the competences of the EU in many different areas and yet one could hardly deny that member states are in a substantial manner still sovereign or respected in their political autonomy. The EU has exclusive competences in the areas of the Customs Union; rules necessary for the functioning of the internal market; monetary policy for euro area countries; conservation of marine biological resources under the Common Fisheries Policy; and common commercial policy. But it has only a shared (with nation states) competence in the single market; employment and social affairs; economic, social, and territorial cohesion; agriculture; fisheries; the environment; consumer protection; transport; trans-European networks; energy; justice and fundamental rights; migration and home affairs; public health; research and space; development cooperation; and humanitarian aid. While all this certainly amounts to a diminution of sovereignty, there are still areas in which member states can exercise their political autonomy.

Jürgen Habermas offers, in two important pieces of writing, a similar reading of Kant's model. He argues that Kant and many of his interpreters start from a false alternative. Between the world republic, that Kant defends in the 1793

"Theory and Practice" essay, and the weak league of nations without coercive powers that he comes to support from 1795 on, there is a neglected middle term that would accommodate Kant's persistent cosmopolitan ambition without any risk of degeneration toward a global autarchy (the famous "soulless despotism"). Suggested by the experience we have "at two hundred years' historical remove" (Habermas 1998) from Kant, this is "a politically constituted global society that reserves institutions and procedures of global governance for states at both the supra- and transnational levels" (Habermas 2006: 135). Major international organizations (the UN, the World Trade Organization [WTO], the EU) exhibit a tendency, still *in fieri*, toward taming state power not through the monopoly of force of a supranational entity such as the world republic or even the "republic of republics," but through the progressive transfer of competencies, previously reserved to the state, to higher institutional bodies. Even if member states remain free to leave the organization (and Brexit proves this is more than a logical possibility) the stability of the supranational organization is strengthened by states' interest in remaining within the organization itself. In other words, as Habermas puts it, the

> democratic federal state writ large – the global state of nations or world republic – is the wrong model. No structural analogy exists between the constitution of a sovereign state that can determine what political competences it claims for itself (and hence possesses supreme constitutional authority), on the one hand, and the constitution of an inclusive world organization that is nevertheless restricted to a few, carefully circumscribed functions, on the other. (Habermas 2006: 134)

The question of what kind of supranational institution Kant's theory of peace needs, quite independently of the form Kant ultimately endorses, is at the center of another influential reading worth considering for its qualified defense of the "world republic" option. In an essay devoted to our theme (Höffe 2004) and in the third part of *Kant's Cosmopolitan Theory of Law and Peace* (Höffe 2006), Otfried Höffe argues that the federation without coercive powers is helplessly insufficient to realize a juridical condition capable of securing an innate right to freedom for all human beings while at the same time delivering lasting peace. Kant's endorsement of the federation is useful only as a reminder that Kant certainly rules out what Höffe calls "an exclusive cosmopolitanism." Only a cosmopolitan order that "does not supplant national civil law, but supplements it" (Höffe 2006: 140) can be considered as a solution. The necessity of a word republic, however, remains. A global institution with some of the powers reserved to states, hence with a minimal state form, is the sole true guarantee of individual spheres of freedom at the global level and of lasting peace. The global institution will have to guarantee the minimal legal equality among individuals sufficient for nondomination. Kant must then accept some analogy between a cosmopolitan legal order and the legal order of a state, but only to a point. Like Habermas, Höffe is keen to emphasize that the analogy between individuals forming a state and states forming a world republic is the wrong way to extend at the international level the duty to create a legal order. In contrast to "primary states," the world republic "is assigned only a narrow range of powers; it is then a minimal world state" organized along republican lines. Such a world republic "demands ceding state sovereignty, but only to a minimal extent" (Höffe 2006: 203). Thus, "the public safeguarding of rights in the legal form" culminates in the task of creating a subsidiary and federal world republic (Höffe 2006: 195).[36]

The debate on the exact kind of institution Kant ultimately wants or should want for reasons of logical consistency and normative credibility (world republic, republic of federated republics, politically constituted global society, league of states with or without coercive powers) is also at the center of Pauline Kleingeld's reading. In a series of publications culminating with her *Kant and Cosmopolitanism* (Kleingeld 2011), Kleingeld rejects the common idea that Kant from 1795 on abandons the international federation with coercive powers as an ideal to be pursued. She holds that while Kant has good reasons to reject the world republic option, he consistently defends the solution of a plurality of federated states. The voluntary league is nothing but a first step in a process toward an international federation with powers and competences far superior to those commonly associated with a loose league (Kleingeld 2006). While Pogge and Habermas assume that the modern dogma of sovereignty blinds Kant to a solution in which states alienate *some* of their sovereignty (mainly the unilateral power to decide when to wage war), but maintain full autonomy in all other political areas, Kleingeld thinks that Kant was not blind at all to this solution: The loose league of state is nothing but a step in an evolution toward a federation gradually and spontaneously taking upon itself more and more competences that were previously reserved to nation states, or better, receiving them as a result of peoples/states deciding freely to transfer them.

By suggesting a provisional role for the federation, this reading harmonizes the *Völkerbund-Völkerstaat* alternative, making the first a preparation for the second. First proposed by Fichte, who considered the federation nothing

---

[36] We do not discuss here the position of cosmopolitan democrats such as Daniel Bell and Daniele Archibugi (Archibugi 2008, Held 1995) but their proposal of a global institution halfway (or somewhere in-between) the federation and the confederation, with again some competences moved to the higher political bodies and others left to nation states, clearly falls in the same intellectual category of the four cosmopolitan positions, discussed in this section.

but an intermediate step (*Mittelzustand*) through which humanity should be able to reach the real target, that is, the world republic (Fichte 1845–6: 433), this reading still has a considerable hearing among contemporary readers. For example, Howard Williams argues that Kant "is both advocating an international state as the ultimate goal, but not advocating it as something to be realized in the immediate or near future. It is an objective to put to the back of our minds, but it is an objective we ought always to have in mind" (Williams 1986: 256).[37] However, crucial to this line of thought is the fact that nation states do not dissolve in the federation with coercive powers. States retain their sovereignty, which at least for Kleingeld includes their right to exit. In the next section I am going to argue that unfortunately the idea of a federation with coercive powers is incompatible with states keeping their sovereignty if states transfer competence as regards the military; and that if states do not do so, then the federation does not contribute to peace significantly more than a loose league does.

7 *Tertium Non Datur*: The Problem with Moderate Cosmopolitanism

Independently of their differences, Pogge, Habermas, Kleingeld, and Höffe all indicate the "enhanced" league or minimal world republic as the solution that Kant could and should have defended. This reading is attractive in that it promises to relax the conceptual dilemma Kant faces between guaranteeing peace through a dissolving of nation states into a world republic (or republic of republics) and preserving a plurality of states through a loose league by renouncing the ideal of a permanent and stable peace. As we saw, Kant never abandoned the idea that the only true guarantor of peace is a world republic or a federation with coercive powers. There is no reason to believe, however, that he ended up advocating for a voluntary league without coercive powers because he "did not/could not" think of the solution of breaking down sovereignty with some competences transferred to a supranational institution and others kept for nation states. Before charging Kant with the inability to see this elegant and convenient solution, one should wonder whether the proposal is truly viable. I will argue that the moderate cosmopolitan solution ignores the depths of the problem Kant is facing. And I further suggest that, in addition to the argument on the moral character of states, the nonviability of this solution is what led Kant to prefer the federation over anything institutionally more ambitious. The crucial point is that when it comes to who decides about using force against

---

[37] Other supporters of the provisional reading are Cheneval (2002), Geismann (1996), and Lutz-Bachmann (1997).

external actors – unfortunately the area that matters most for a theory of international peace – a state may not compromise on its *exclusive* competence, if it has to remain sovereign at all.

The point can be proven theoretically and illustrated through one very significant case study. Theoretically, it is sufficient to notice that any transfer of competences by a state to a higher body remains provisional as long as the state retains full sovereignty over its own defense policy, or, which is the same thing, over the use of force toward external actors. Military force is the last thing a state may appeal to in case it wishes to exercise its will against that of others, be they lower, higher, or same-level institutional bodies, partners within an organization, or nonstate actors, and so on. Think of a state as part of an international organization that is either unsatisfied with a certain interpretation of the rules of that organization or simply no longer wants to remain a member. Further imagine that it declares its intentions, but remains unheard by the organization at large and/or by its partners. How could it exercise its will if it does not control an army that could at least threaten the use of violence against opposing actors? Without full control of the army, there is no sovereignty, not even partially.

A major empirical confirmation of the theoretical point above comes from the history of EU's integration process. The EU is particularly significant as a case study because it is the closest thing we have to the enhanced federation favored by moderate cosmopolitans. As Hueglin and Fenna argue, its "institutional framework has evolved gradually but steadily from *intergovernmentalism* to *supranationalism*" (Hueglin and Fenna 2015: 5), thus making the EU closer and closer to a federal, as opposed to confederal, body, in fact, as a case of the success of federalism. They continue:

> Some policy areas remain in the domain of member-state sovereignty, while others have reached the level of full political integration. This resembles the division of powers in federal states. Legislation now almost invariably requires co-decision by two bodies: the Council of Ministers and the European Parliament. This resembles bicameral or dual representation in federal states. As is the case in most of the established federal states as well, the EU practices a system of revenue sharing and redistribution; its regulations have direct effect on member states, citizens, and corporations; a high court, the European Court of Justice, not only adjudicates compliance with EU laws and regulations but, moreover, has acquired powers of judicial review.
>
> (Hueglin and Fenna 2015: 5)

In order to appreciate how sovereignty and exclusive competence on defense policy are indissolubly connected, it is instructive to look at the EU's continued failure to establish, beyond proclamations and good intentions, a common defense policy. Despite its "gradual but steady" progress toward federalism, and despite repeated efforts and some progress made at an incredibly slow pace if compared with economic and monetary integration, the Union still lacks a common voice in foreign relations and, most importantly, in matters related to the use of force.[38] The Treaty on European Union does give the EU competence to define and implement a common foreign and security policy (CSDP), including the progressive framing of a common defense policy. And yet it is the European Council and the Council of the European Union (Article 42 TEU) that take the decisions relating to the CSDP. These two collegiate bodies, respectively the forum of member states' prime ministers and the forum of competent officials (ministers, ambassadors) from the executive of each member state, make decisions *normally by unanimity*, which obviously means that each state normally retains full sovereignty.

If one looks at the history of past attempts to achieve better integration in the matter of defense, the picture is rather clear. Europeans have tried many times to go beyond mere coordination in military affairs and parallel the economic, monetary and to a certain extent political integration they were building in the post–World War II era. And yet, something has always gone wrong, and never by accident. We start with France's refusal to ratify the European Defence Community (EDC) in 1954. As noticed by Rosato, "Sovereignty concerns . . . meant that the defense community was never particularly popular in France. . . . The preexisting NATO system was far preferable on this score: although it was tightly organized for operational purposes, the United States, Britain, and France retained sovereignty over their own forces" (Rosato 2011: 63). While economic and monetary integration progressed in the years leading to the collapse of the Soviet Union, with the consolidation of an internal market over and beyond a custom-free zone, military integration languished, aggravated by the evaporation of the major geopolitical factor (the threat posed by the USSR) that could have provided an impetus to create an integrated defense. Indeed, with the USSR gone, Europeans felt confident enough to establish a common defense policy for the first time independently of their American ally, which in practical terms meant the creation of a structure that was an alternative to NATO. But again, its results were limited.

At the 1999 Helsinki summit, European leaders appeared to have taken decisive steps in this direction, contingently motivated by the way in which the air strike in Kosovo conducted by NATO forces, notably the United States, painfully exposed the inability of the EU to back up its diplomatic and negotiating efforts with adequate military power. This led to the creation of the European Security and

---

[38] For a thorough, perhaps at times ungenerous, and yet by-and-large correct analysis of the EU as a would-be world power, see Majone (2009).

Defence Policy (ESDP), which was renamed the Common Security and Defence Policy (CSDP) in 2009 by the Treaty of Lisbon. The CSDP was further developed in 2016 with a global strategy for the foreign and security policy of the EU, designed by EU leaders in the aftermath of the Russian annexation of Crimea, Brexit, and Trump's promise to diminish the US's military commitment within NATO.

What were the results of this effort at a common defense policy? It would be unfair to claim that the EU is wholly absent in the international arena. Since 1999 the EU has launched thirty-four missions and operations in fields ranging from conflict prevention through peacemaking, peacekeeping, crisis management, joint disarmament operations, and military advice and assistance to post-conflict stabilization. Currently, the EU is present on three continents through the deployment of ten civilian and six military missions. Yet even the most ardent fan of the EU knows that (a) the intergovernmental nature of the EU defense has never been overcome; (b) even today the EU is unable to show a united military power capable of working as leverage in what are currently the hottest contexts, even those clearly falling within its sphere of influence (just think of Turkey and Russia gaining control and influence in the Middle East and North Africa); (c) after seventy years of good intentions and fanfare, and despite the creation of structures such as the Permanent Structured Cooperation (PESCO), the European Defence Fund (EDF), and the High Representative of the Union for Foreign Affairs and Security Policy, we are not even close to anything resembling a Europe with a common voice in foreign affairs and a common army to back it up.

This less-than-exciting outcome cannot be accounted for in terms of chance or geopolitical considerations working against the result of a common European defense. If the fall of the Soviet Union removed one pressing reason to unite against a common threat, we have come far enough to have reasons to be threatened by new autocratic powers (mainly Russia with its quasi-satellite states such as Belarus, and China), and yet this is not sufficient to move beyond enhanced cooperation to true integration. One major reason, if not the reason for this is that member states can renounce full control of the use of force only by forfeiting the last and deepest level of national sovereignty. Such a move would end the EU as we know it and turn it, to the joy of many past and present continental federalists, into something like the United States of Europe. As long as there is an alternative way of guaranteeing security – and NATO provides such an alternative – European states will never move beyond fanfare about military integration, because they know that this is the only way to avoid their end as independent political entities.[39]

---

[39] Sebastian Rosato makes a similar point. Starting from a perspective on international relations largely inspired by realism, he argues that the EU's failure to establish a military union is due to the fact that European member states do not want to give up their sovereignty. They would be

The lesson one should learn at this point is quite evident. Kant *consistently* ended up favoring the solution of the voluntary league, given that he wanted, like moderate cosmopolitans, to avoid the merging of all states into one. The league does not provide any guarantee of peace and yet it is to be preferred because it does not erode the deepest layer of sovereignty of states. Moreover, while unable to provide a guarantee of peace, the league is still a significant peace factor because it constitutes a permanent channel of diplomatic relations where states can have their controversies discussed and assessed by something like a third independent party, even if this judicial authority may have no ultimate power to enforce its decisions (a reluctant state may simply leave the federation if it refuses to comply). The contemporary experience of many intergovernmental organizations (IGOs), mixed or fully democratic, from the Arab League to the Assocation of Southeast Asian Nations (ASEAN), the Organization of American States (OAS), and the African Union (AU), proves precisely how institutions of this kind can do *something* to mediate controversies between members, even if they are in no position to prevent war in all circumstances. This limited contribution to peace would of course increase its own impact to the extent to which the other two factors of Kant's model make progress, that is, members of the voluntary league become republican and economic and cultural interdependencies among them grow, thereby making war very costly, like in the case of the EU. While Kant never abandoned the idea that a guarantee of perpetual peace requires the full overcoming of the international state of nature in perfect analogy with the domestic case, he came to realize that states are not merely self-interested entities stubbornly refusing to comply with what practical reason demands. They are not mere "accidents," as the Reflexion cited above nicely illustrates. They have a moral personality ultimately resting on the juridical condition that was created the moment (no matter how imaginary and hypothetical) in which a formerly scattered group of individuals followed the first-order command of practical reason, abandoned their specific (domestic) state of nature, and created a commonwealth. Their choice and the specific manner in which their freedoms and rights were (more or less) secured within that specific state deserve moral and political respect. Normative/moral, not merely pragmatic reasons set limits to the analogy between the domestic and the international case.

This is obviously compatible with the possibility that states *freely* decide to dissolve themselves to enter either a world republic or a federal state of states. This is the limited amount of overlapping that my reading has with the

---

ready to do so only if no alternative way to guarantee security were available. But NATO still provides this alternative (Rosato 2011: 46).

above-discussed provisional reading sponsored by Fichte, Kleingeld, Williams, and others. The point we share is that nothing in Kant prevents the possibility of a free and uncoerced overcoming of the international system in favor of some form of the world state. In fact, much in his philosophy encourages this development. The difference between my reading and the others is that I do not think that the problem is merely one of insufficient moral education on the parts of political leaders and/or citizens. In my reading, citizens of a state who refuse to dissolve their nation into some higher authority are not morally defective, because they can make the argument that what they are defending was generated by compliance with the first-level command of practical reason. Hence, it is entirely within the legitimate scope of their freedom to reject the dissolution of their nation.

This difference has consequences for the different way in which I read the possibility of a spontaneous and free overcoming of nation states in favor of the world republic or other forms of cosmopolitan authority. While champions of the provisional reading are rather elusive on the conditions that must be met to make such a move legitimate, I argue that such conditions must be spelled out carefully and are rather demanding. Here a comparison with a recent discussion in the theory of human rights may prove instructive. Many experts today argue that human rights should make room for a people's choice of a nondemocratic form of government. Thomas Christiano, for example, thinks that instrumental and intrinsic considerations suggest that there is a human right to democracy, understood as a right to perfect civil and political equality (Christiano 2015). At the same time, however, a state may choose to adopt a nondemocratic form of government without violating that individual right, but with a very demanding condition: *All* citizens (not a majority) need to waive their right to democracy. I wonder whether something similar holds for the decision to dissolve a state. The original decision of a people to form a state may be compatible with a later decision to dissolve it. But what kind of majority would be necessary for that? A simple one with at least 50 percent voter turnout? A qualified one? A vote that is unanimous, at least in principle, in the sense that there are reasons to believe that those opposing the dissolution are somehow wrong? Certainly, from a Kantian perspective, there should be clear reasons to believe that the decision springs from the general will, not from the interests of one faction, no matter how large.

At this point moderate cosmopolitans may argue that the general will cannot fail to endorse a decision that would guarantee the security of all citizens of the state. And yet, this would problematically blur any distinction between universal practical reason and the general will of each domestic context. The latter, taking into considerations its Rousseauian pedigree, is after the common good of a people, not of humanity.[40] And as long as the will of a people favors a condition of local political autonomy over one of certainty about world peace, it would be hard to construe this preference necessarily as the preference of a faction or as the unanimous yet inauthentic decision inspired by the *volonté des tous*.

Cosmopolitans could also legitimately protest that the case under consideration is not different than the one applying to individuals before the constitution of the state. If they have a duty to establish a domestic state to preserve freedom and peace, and if they can be forced to enter one even if they are unwilling to do so, are they not under the same duty to move one step up and complete the transition toward a cosmopolitan condition in which the state of nature is finally overcome, not only internally but also externally? If the decision is ultimately that of individuals and not of the states to which they belong, are we not back to the possibility of coercing even those individuals who refuse to take the last step necessary for the establishment of a true cosmopolitan condition? Possibly so. We touch here what has been aptly described by Katrin Flikschuh as the sovereignty dilemma of Kant's notion of international right. To this last point of our analysis, I now turn.

8 The "Sovereignty Dilemma" Reconsidered

Flikschuh notices a "sovereignty dilemma" affecting Kant's notion of international right. For Kant, right is analytically connected to coercion. Moreover, sovereign states are the exclusive and supreme agents in charge of enforcing right. Hence they cannot be legitimately coerced by other states or supra-state institutions to enter a federation and to abide by the rules of its membership with no option to abandon it. At the same time, in the domain of international relations practical reason prescribes that states establish an international juridical condition as a necessary component of justice. Therefore, concludes Flikschuh, "Kant's theory of Right simultaneously requires and prohibits the juridical compulsion of states" (Flikschuh 2010: 471). Flikschuh further suggests that the dilemma can only be solved if we move away from the logic of analogy/disanalogy between the domestic and the international case, and focus on the fact that in Kant, right is a system in which each part (domestic, international, or cosmopolitan) cannot stand without the others. If we assume this perspective, then the domestic component cannot do without the other

---

[40] Ferrara has a similar idea, inspired by Rawls' global public reason, when he speaks of a freestanding, political notion of "the good of humanity" capturing what would be "most reasonable" for human beings to accept as constitutional essentials of a global state (Ferrara and Michelman 2021: 148–52).

international and cosmopolitan right. This means that states cannot welcome the unlimited sovereignty that right assigns to them while ignoring the demands the very same right puts upon them at the international and cosmopolitan level. If right is a system made of three interdependent components, states cannot, so to speak, pick and choose among them.

This is an interesting reading but, by the light of what we have already observed, the sovereignty dilemma does not seem to get to the heart of the problem that Kant is confronting. The fact that states can never be coerced from the outside is obviously compatible, as we saw, with the possibility that they freely decide to transfer some of their competences to the supranational institution. This is indeed what Flikschuh suggests they can and should do to avoid the "picking and choosing" described above. But Kant's real and more profound dilemma is that if states renounce or diminish – even freely – their exclusive competence in one particular area – the use of force toward external actors, which is the competence that *must* be transferred if war is to be overcome – they simply are no longer sovereign.

Notice that this point is not dependent on a Weberian conception of sovereignty as a monopoly of force, because Weber himself thought that *in certain areas* the state may allow its exclusive authority to be limited without compromising its sovereignty. One must subscribe even less to a Schmittian conception, which rests on the ability to declare the state of exception (*Ausnahmezustand*). Rather, the point is a Hobbesian one, with an important qualification. For Hobbes, a soverign state is one that keeps ultimate authority over deciding whether the terms of whatever agreement it has entered have been respected. We share this conception and qualify it by noticing that this is equivalent to saying that the state is sovereign if it keeps ultimate control over the force that it may need to use to counter any action by an external agent perceived as either violating existing agreements or posing an existential threat. A state is sovereign if it keeps *exclusive* competence over the use of force toward external actors (be they other states or supranational institutions). If it loses that competence and yet still reacts to a perceived injustice, its reaction can only be conceptualized as a violent rebellion *within a state*. In other words, we would already be in a world state or in a federal state of states.

This notion of sovereignty, which, I am suggesting, Kant endorses, is in stark contrast with the necessity, to which Kant also subscribes, of a supranational institution *with* coercive powers (the point emphasized in particular by Höffe), which obviously implies that states may not have at their disposal a military force to counter the supranational institution. In this sense, far more radical than the one suggested by Flikschuh, Kant's conception of right simultaneously requires and prohibits the juridical compulsion of states. Only if the depths of the paradox are fully appreciated can one understand fully the normative reasons that led the mature Kant (a) to abandon what he kept on believing his entire life was the *sole* true solution to the problem of war (on this point Byrd and Hruschka are right) and (b) to endorse the limited diplomatic contribution to peace offered by the "permanent congress of states." To save the plurality of states Kant came to believe that one needs to be satisfied with the difference (small or big, this is debatable) made by the diplomatic channels offered by the loose league, while hoping that the league's contribution be magnified and rendered sufficient by the combined effect of the other two peace-promoting factors: republicanism inside states and cosmopolitan right.   .

In a sense, Thomas Pogge is right that the EU is a good example of the Kantian federation. It is the best example, however, because its attempt to further the process of integration and to extend it to the creation of a truly common defense while remaining a confederation of sovereign states mirrors the paradox with which Kant struggled in all of his political writings. The fact that he did not solve it completely and that his praise for the "rational" solution of the world state ultimately coexists with his preference for the federation is not a sign of intellectual weakness, even less of political cowardice. It reflects something that one could describe as a sort of antinomy of practical-political reason.

9 Concluding Remarks

Kant's model of perpetual peace is still one of the most influential paradigms at our disposal in terms of thinking of world affairs and imagining political solutions to the most pressing issues of our time. The model changes in the hands of Kant over time, and behind its apparent simplicity lurk tensions and dilemmas, some of which I tried to highlight and, to the extent possible, solve. Among those that are particularly fascinating is Kant's changing attitude toward the nature, shape, and powers (or lack thereof) of the supranational institution that plays the role of second pillar of the entire model. I suggested that Kant saw with absolute clarity a dilemma that was growing within his system of right between the never-abandoned belief that the sole solution of war is the overcoming of states and the necessity of respecting the "posited" moral personality of states, established at the moment in which a scattered group of individuals obeyed practical reason's command to move from a lawless condition to one in which the inborn right(s) of human beings would be secured. I suggested that this dilemma could only be overcome if citizens of the existing nations unanimously decided to dissolve their states to merge into a global compound (it does not matter whether in the form of a single universal republic or in that of an only apparently less stringent federal state of states). In Kantian terms this would mean that the general will of each domestic republic would merge into a sort of global general will that decides to win peace at the cost of local political autonomy. Despite the principled preference for the federation, whose profound ground I highlighted above, nothing in Kant's system prevents this evolution.

The only problem with this – it seems to me – is the rather demanding condition on which the passage would remain respectful of the rights of citizens of each existing state. I suggested that this condition is their *principled* unanimous consensus: All citizens should be able to agree, not just a majority. One could be puzzled by this suggestion, which of course merely tries to guess what Kant would or should say, given his silence on the point: the recent referendum held in Scotland to leave the UK proves that even decisions about the survival of nations and the birth of new entities *are* taken by simple majorities. Similarly, very few would object if a new referendum held in Kosovo and Albania established, against the will of some Kosovars, that the two states merge.

While it is true that Kant allows for decisions made by political actors without the explicit support of the people – think of the single-handed decision of an enlightened ruling class to transform a despotic state into a republic or to change the form of sovereignty to bring government more ino line with the spirit of the original contract (MS 6:340) – by his standards the decision to merge the state into a higher body would seem to be an altogether different decision. It would call into question the pact that individuals subscribed to when they followed the first-order command of practical reason and overcame their domestic state of nature. When they did that, they generated a rightful condition that is hard to conceptualize as one that could be overcome by coercing some unwilling individuals. They may oppose it by appealing to the terms of the original pact to which they subscribed. To be sure, practical reason now commands that states be dissolved because this is the unique manner to *guarantee* peace. It could also be said that the principled unanimous consensus I so much insist on is less demanding than it sounds. All citizens *should* agree to it, were their moral insight sharp enough. Or they *would* agree to the merging, were they set in an ideal condition of choice. Possibly so, and yet some doubts remain.

References

Anderson-Gold, S. (2006). Cosmopolitan Right Kant's Key to Perpetual Peace. In L. Caranti, ed., *Kant's Perpetual Peace: New Interpretative Essays*. Rome: Luiss University Press, pp. 137–47.

Archibugi, D. (1995). Immanuel Kant, Cosmopolitan Law, and Peace. *European Journal of International Relations*, 1(4), 429–56.

Archibugi, D. (2008). *The Global Commonwealth of Citizens: Toward Cosmopolitan Democracy*. Princeton, NJ: Princeton University Press.

Archibugi, D. & Beetham, D. (1998). *Diritti umani e democrazia cosmopolita*. Milan: Feltrinelli.

Axinn, S. (1989). Kant on World Government. In G. Funcke and T. M. Seebohm, eds., *Proceedings: Sixth International Kant Congress*: Washington, DC: University Press of America, pp. 243–51.

Bobbio, N. (2005). Introduzione. In I. Kant, ed., *Per la pace perpetua*. Rome: Editori Riuniti, pp. x–xxv.

Brito Vieira, M. (2017). Introduction. In M.Brito Vieira, ed., *Reclaiming Representation*. London: Routledge, pp. 1–21.

Brown, G. W. (2005). State Sovereignty, Federation and Kantian Cosmopolitanism. *European Journal of International Relations*, 11(4), 495–522. DOI:https://doi.org/10.1177/1354066105057898.

Brown, G. W. (2009). *Grounding Cosmopolitanism: From Kant to the Idea of a Cosmopolitan Constitution*. Edinburgh: Edinburgh University Press.

Bull, H. (1977). *The Anarchical Society: A Study of Order in World Politics*. London: Macmillan.

Byrd, B. S. & Hruschka, J. (2010). *Kant's Doctrine of Right: A Commentary*. Cambridge: Cambridge University Press.

Caranti, L. (2006). Perpetual War for Perpetual Peace? Reflections on the Realist Critique of Kant's Project. *Journal of Human Rights*, 18(3), 23–45.

Caranti. L. (2012). Kant's Theory of Human Rights. In T. Cushman, ed., *Handbook of Human Rights*. Abingdon: Routledge, pp. 35–44.

Caranti, L. (2014). The Guarantee of Perpetual Peace: Three Concerns. In A. Goldman, T.TT. Patrone, & P. Formosa, eds., *Politics and Teleology in Kant*. Cardiff: University of Wales Press, pp. 145–62.

Caranti, L. (2016). Kantian Peace and Liberal Peace: Three Concerns. *Journal of Political Philosophy*, 24(4), 446–69.

Caranti, L. (2017a). *Kant's Politics Today: Human Rights, Peace, Progress*. Cardiff: University of Wales Press.

Caranti, L. (2017b). How Cosmopolitanism Reduces Conflict: Narrow and Broad Readings of Kant's Third Ingredient for Peace. *Journal of International Political Theory*, 14(1), 1–18.

Caranti, L. (2018). The Kantian Federation: Two Hermeneutical Problems. In H. Klemme & A. Falduto, eds., *Kant und seine Kritiker*. Hildesheim: Olms Weidemann, pp. 347–62.

Caranti, L. (2022). Kant *via* Rousseau against Democracy. In L. Caranti & A. Pinzani, eds., *Kant and the Problem of Politics in the Contemporary World*. London: Routledge.

Carson, Thomas L. (1988). *Perpetual Peace*. What Kant Should Have Said. *Social Theory and Practice* 14(2) (Summer), 173–214.

Cavallar, G. (1999). *Kant and the Theory of Practice*. Vienna: Böhlau.

Cavallar, G. (2002). *The Rights of Strangers: Theories of International Hospitality*. New York: Routledge.

Cavallar, G. (2015). *Kant's Embedded Cosmopolitanism: History, Philosophy and Education for World Citizens*. Berlin: De Gruyter.

Cavallar, G. (2020). *Kant and the Theory and Practice of International Right*. Cardiff: University of Wales Press.

Cheneval F. (2002). *Philosophie in Weltbürgerlicher Bedeutung: Über die Entstehung und die Philosophischen Grundlagen des Supranationalen und Kosmopolitischen Denkens der Moderne*. Basel: Schwabe.

Christiano, T. (2015). Self-Determination and the Human Right to Democracy. In R. Cruft, M. S. Liao, & M. Renzo, eds., *Philosophical Foundations of Human Rights*. Oxford: Oxford University Press, pp. 459–80.

Covell, C. (1998). *Kant and the Law of Peace: A Study in the Philosophy of Law and International Relations*, Houndmills: Macmillan-Saint Martin's Press.

Derrida, J. (2000). *Of Hospitality*. Stanford, CA: Stanford University Press.

Doyle, M. W. (1983a). Kant, Liberal Legacies, and Foreign Affairs (Part I). *Philosophy and Public Affairs*, 12(3), 205–35.

Doyle, M. W. (1983b). Kant, Liberal Legacies, and Foreign Affairs (Part II). *Philosophy and Public Affairs*, 12(4), 323–53.

Doyle, M. W. (2012). *Liberal Peace*. Abingdon: Routledge.

Ebbinghaus, J. (1968). Kants Lehre vom ewigen Frieden und die Kriegsschuldfrage. In J. Ebbinghaus, *Gesammelte Aufsätze, Vorträge und Reden*. Hildesheim: Olms.

Eberl, O. & Niesen, P. (2011). *Immanuel Kant: Zum ewigen Frieden und Auszüge aus der Rechtslehre: Kommentar*. Berlin: Suhrkamp.

Ferrara, A. & Michelman, F. I. (2022). *Legitimation by Constitution*. Oxford: Oxford University Press.

Fichte, J. G. (1845–6). *Zum Ewigen Frieden: Ein Philosophischer Entwurf von Immanuel Kant*. In I. H. Fichte, ed., *Sämmtliche Werke*, 4 vols. Berlin: Veit & Comp.

Fleischacker, S. (1996). Values behind the Market: Kant's Response to the *Wealth of Nations*. *History of Political Thought*, 57, 379–407.

Flikschuh, K. (2010). Kant's Sovereignty Dilemma: A Contemporary Analysis. *The Journal of Political Philosophy*, 18(4), 469–93.

Friedrich, Carl J. (1948). *Inevitable Peace*. Cambridge, MA: Harvard University Press.

Gallie, W. B. (1978). *Philosophers of Peace and War: Kant, Clausewitz, Marx, Engels and Tolstoy*. Cambridge: Cambridge University Press.

Geismann, G. (1996). Kant on Eternal Peace. In K. G. Ballestrem, V. Gerhardt, H. Ottmann, and M. P. Thompson, eds., *Politisches Denken Jahrbuch 1995/96*. Stuttgart: J.B. Metzler. DOI:https://doi.org/10.1007 /978-3-476-03633-9_11.

Gerhardt, V. (1995). *Immanuel Kants Entwurf "Zum Ewigen Frieden."* Darmstadt: Wissenschaftliche Buchgesellschaft.

Gilens, M. & Page, B. I. (2017). *Democracy in America? What Has Gone Wrong and What We Can Do About It*. Chicago: University of Chicago Press.

Gutmann, A. & Thompson, D. (2004). *Why Deliberative Democracy?* Princeton, NJ: Princeton University Press.

Guyer, P. (2006). The Possibility of Perpetual Peace. In L. Caranti, ed., *Kant's Perpetual Peace: New Interpretative Essays*. Rome: Luiss University Press, pp. 161–82.

Guyer, P. (2019). Luigi Caranti's *Kant's Political Legacy*. *Kantian Review*, 24 (2), 275–88.

Habermas, J. (1998). *The Inclusion of the Other: Studies in Political Theory*. Cambridge, MA: MIT Press.

Habermas, J. (2006). *The Divided West*. Cambridge, MA: Polity Press.

Held, D. (1995). *Democracy and the Global Order*. Cambridge, MA: Polity Press.

Hinsley, F. H. (1963). *Power and Pursuit of Peace: Theory and Practice in the History of Relations between the States*. Cambridge: Cambridge University Press.

Höffe, O. (2004). Völkerbund oder Weltrepublik? In O. Höffe. ed., *Immanuel Kant: Zum Ewigen Frieden*. Berlin: Akademie Verlag, pp. 109–32.

Höffe, O. (2006). *Kant's Cosmopolitan Theory of Law and Peace*. Cambridge: Cambridge University Press.

Hueglin, T.O. & Fenna, A. (2015). *Comparative Federalism. A Systematic Inquiry*. Toronto: University of Toronto Press.

International Commission on Intervention and State Sovereignty (ICISS). (2001). *The Responsibility to Protect: Report of the International*

Commission on Intervention and State Sovereignty. Ottawa: International Development Research Centre for ICISS.

Kersting, W. (1996). Weltfriedensordnung und globale Verteilungsgerechtigkeit: Kants Konzeption eines vollständigen Rechtsfriedens und diegegenwärtige politische Philosophie der internationalen Beziehungen. In R. Merkel and R. Wittmann, eds., *Zum ewigen Frieden: Grundlagen, Aktualität und Aussichten einer Idee von Immanuel Kant.* Frankfurt: Suhrkamp, pp. 172–212.

Kleingeld, P. (2006). Kant's Argument's for the League of States. In L. Caranti, ed., *Kant's Perpetual Peace: New Interpretative Essays.* Rome: Luiss University Press, pp. 55–74.

Kleingeld, P. (2011). *Kant and Cosmopolitanism.* Cambridge: Cambridge University Press.

Losurdo, D. (1983). *Autocensura e Compromesso nel Pensiero Politico di Kant.* Naples: Istituto Italiano per gli Studi Filosofici, Bibliopolis.

Ludwig, B. (2006). Condemned to Peace: What Does Nature Guarantee in Kant's Treatise of Eternal Peace? In L. Caranti (ed.), *Kant's Perpetual Peace: New Interpretative Essays.* Rome: Luiss University Press, pp. 183–95.

Lutz-Bachmann M. (1997). Kant's Idea of Peace and the Philosophical Conception of a World Republic. In J. Bohman & M. Lutz-Bachman, eds., *Perpetual Peace: Essays on Kant's Cosmopolitan Ideal.* Cambridge, MA: MIT University Press, pp. 59–77.

MacMillan, J. (1995). A Kantian Protest Against the Peculiar Discourse of Inter-Liberal State Peace. *Millennium,* 24(3), 549–62.

Majone, G. (2009). *Europe As the Would-Be World Power: The EU at Fifty.* Cambridge, MA: Cambridge University Press.

Manin, B. (1997). *The Principles of Representative Government.* Cambridge: Cambridge University Press.

Marini, G. (1998). Il diritto cosmopolitico nel progetto kantiano per la pace perpetua con particolare riferimento al secondo articolo definitivo. In G. Marini, *Tre studi sul cosmopolitismo.* Pisa: Istituti Editoriali e Poligrafici Internazionali, pp. 25–39.

Marini, G. (2001). Per una repubblica federale mondiale. In G. M. Chiodi, R. Gatti, and G. Marini, eds., *La filosofia politica di Kant: Seminarioperugino per lo studio dei classici.* Milan: Angeli, pp. 19–34.

Mikalsen, K. K. (2019). Kantian Republicanism in the International Sphere: Equal Sovereignty As a Condition of Global Justice. In G. Wallace Brown & Á. Telegdi-Csetri, eds., *Kant's Cosmopolitics: Contemporary Issues and Global Debates.* Edinburgh: Edinburgh University Press, pp. 15–26.

Mori, M. (2008). *La Pace e la Ragione: Kant e le Relazioni Internazionali. Politica, Diritto, Storia*. Bologna: Il Mulino.

Mulholland, L. A. (1987). Kant on War and International Justice. *Kant Studien*, 78, 25–41.

Nida-Rümelin, J. (1996). Ewiger Friede zwischen Moralismus und Hobbesianismus. In R. Merkel & R. Wittmann, eds., *Zum Ewiger Frieden: Grundlagen, Aktualität und Aussichten einer Idee von Immanuel Kant*. Frankfurt: Suhrkamp, pp. 239–55.

Philonenko, A. (1988). Kant et le problème de la paix. In A. Philonenko (ed.), *Essais sur la philosophie de la guerre*. Paris: Vrin, pp. 26–42.

Pinzani, A. (2008). Representation in Kant's Political Theory. In J. Joerden, S. Byrd, & J. Hruschka, eds., *Jahrbuch für Recht und Ethik 16*. Berlin: Duncker & Humblot, pp. 203–26.

Pitkin, Hanna F. (1967). *The Concept of Representation*. Berkeley: University of California Press.

Pogge, T. (2006). Kant's Vision, Europe, and a Global Federation. In L. Caranti, ed., *Kant's Perpetual Peace: New Interpretative Essays*. Rome: LUISS University Press, pp. 75–96.

Rawls, J. (1999). *The Law of Peoples*. Cambridge, MA: Harvard University Press.

Ripstein, A. (2009). *Force and Freedom*. Totowa, NJ: Rowman & Littlefield.

Ripstein, A. (2016). Just War, Regular War, and Perpetual Peace. *Kant-Studien*, 107(1), 179–95. DOI: https://doi.org/10.1515/kant-2016-0009

Ripstein, A. (2021). *Rules for Wrongdoers: Law, Morality, War*. Oxford: Oxford University Press.

Roff, H. M. (2015). *Global Justice, Kant and the Responsibility to Protect: A Provisional Duty*. London: Routledge.

Rosato, S. (2011). Europe's Troubles: Power Politics and the State of the European Project. *International Security*, 35(4), 45–86.

Rosen, A. D. (1993). *Kant's Theory of Justice*. Ithaca, NY: Cornell University Press.

Rosenbaum, D. E. (2004). A Closer Look at Cheney and Halliburton. *The New York Times*, September 28. www.nytimes.com/2004/09/28/us/a-closer-look-at-cheney-and-halliburton.html

Russett, B. (2005). Bushwhacking the Democratic Peace. *International Studies Perspectives*, 6(4), 395–408.

Ruyssen, T. (1924). Les origines kantiennes de la société Des nations. *Revue de Métaphysique et de Morale* 31(2), 355–71.

Taraborrelli, A. (2006). Reflections on Kant's Third Definitive Article of "Perpetual Peace." In L. Caranti, ed., *Kant's Perpetual Peace: New Interpretative Essays*. Rome: LUISS University Press, pp. 133–42.

Tesòn, F. (1992). The Kantian Theory of International Law. *Columbia Law Review*, 53, 53–102.

Thompson, K. (2008). Sovereignty, hospitality, and commerce: Kant and cosmopolitan right. *Jahrbuch fur Recht und Ethik* 16, 305–19.

Urbinati, N. (2000). Representation as Advocacy: A Study of Democratic Deliberation. *Political Theory*, 28(6), 758–86.

Williams, H. (1986). *Kant's Political Philosophy.* New York: St. Martin's Press.

Williams, H. (1992). Kant's Optimism in his Social and Political Theory. In H. Williams, ed., *Essays on Kant's Political Philosophy.* Cardiff: University of Wales Press, pp. 1–14.

Waldron, J. (2000) What is Cosmopolitan? *Journal of Political Philosophy* 8(2), 227–43.

Wood, A. (1995). Kant's Project for Perpetual Peace. In H. Robinson, ed., *Proceedings of the Eighth International Kant Congress*, Vol. 1. Milwaukee, WI: Marquette University Press, pp. 3–18.

Acknowledgments

I would like to express my gratitude to the three editors of this Elements series devoted to the philosophy of Immanuel Kant (Desmond Hogan, Howard Williams, and Allen Wood) for entrusting me with the task of introducing the reader to Kant's model of peace in general and to his view of the federation in particular, while discussing some of the numerous challenges interpreters have encountered. Special thanks go to friends and colleagues who read and cogently commented on earlier versions of the essay: Paul Guyer, Frederick Rauscher, Peter Niesen, Pauline Kleingeld, Alessandro Ferrara, and Thomas Pogge.

The Philosophy of Immanuel Kant

Desmond Hogan
Princeton University
Desmond Hogan joined the philosophy department at Princeton in 2004. His interests include Kant, Leibniz and German rationalism, early modern philosophy, and questions about causation and freedom. Recent work includes 'Kant on Foreknowledge of Contingent Truths', *Res Philosophica* 91 (1) (2014); 'Kant's Theory of Divine and Secondary Causation', in Brandon Look (ed.) *Leibniz and Kant*, Oxford University Press (forthcoming); 'Kant and the Character of Mathematical Inference', in Carl Posy and Ofra Rechter (eds.), *Kant's Philosophy of Mathematics Vol. I*, Cambridge University Press (2020).

Howard Williams
University of Cardiff
Howard Williams was appointed Honorary Distinguished Professor at the Department of Politics and International Relations, University of Cardiff in 2014. He is also Emeritus Professor in Political Theory at the Department of International Politics, Aberystwyth University, a member of the Coleg Cymraeg Cenedlaethol (Welsh-language national college) and a Fellow of the Learned Society of Wales. He is the author of *Marx* (1980); *Kant's Political Philosophy* (1983); *Concepts of Ideology* (1988); *Hegel, Heraclitus and Marx's Dialectic* (1989); *International Relations in Political Theory* (1992); *International Relations and the Limits of Political Theory* (1996); *Kant's Critique of Hobbes: Sovereignty and Cosmopolitanism* (2003); *Kant and the End of War* (2012) and is currently editor of the journal *Kantian Review*. He is writing a book on the Kantian legacy in political philosophy for a new series edited by Paul Guyer.

Allen Wood
Indiana University
Allen Wood is Ward W. and Priscilla B. Woods Professor Emeritus at Stanford University. He was a John S. Guggenheim Fellow at the Free University in Berlin, a National Endowment for the Humanities Fellow at the University of Bonn and Isaiah Berlin Visiting Professor at the University of Oxford. He is on the editorial board of eight philosophy journals, five book series and *The Stanford Encyclopedia of Philosophy*. Along with Paul Guyer, Professor Wood is co-editor of The Cambridge Edition of the Works of Immanuel Kant and translator of the *Critique of Pure Reason*. He is the author or editor of a number of other works, mainly on Kant, Hegel and Karl Marx. His most recently published books are *Fichte's Ethical Thought*, Oxford University Press (2016) and *Kant and Religion*, Cambridge University Press (2020). Wood is a member of the American Academy of Arts and Sciences.

About the Series
This Cambridge Elements series provides an extensive overview of Kant's philosophy and its impact upon philosophy and philosophers. Distinguished Kant specialists provide an up-to-date summary of the results of current research in their fields and give their own take on what they believe are the most significant debates influencing research, drawing original conclusions.

Cambridge Elements ≡

The Philosophy of Immanuel Kant

Printed in the United States
by Baker & Taylor Publisher Services